ADDITIONAL PRAISE FOR *ART WORKS*

"*Art Works* tells the complicated and fascinating story of the recent history of activism and the arts and points to new ways in which the arts, pop culture, and institutions are aligning themselves to address issues of violence, beauty, capitalism, and justice. Challenging and inspiring, the book raises many fundamental questions about the purpose of art and its relationship to societal change."

—Laurie Anderson

"*Art Works*, or it can with the right allies, the right audiences, and the right amounts of love and anger. Coming from outside the mainstream art world, Ken Grossinger's book is an invaluable source for activist artists looking to increase their social impact."

—Lucy R. Lippard, author of *Get the Message? A Decade of Art for Social Change*

"President Kennedy spoke of the role of art to 'nourish the soul.' In this new book, Ken Grossinger shows us how the arts can inspire, ennoble, challenge, and sustain the soul of our democracy."

—Paul Begala, political commentator

"This is a book of my own heart, a road map celebrating the explosive fusion of art and activism. *Art Works* in transforming consciousness and inspiring the highest good."

—V (formerly Eve Ensler)

"Ken Grossinger has written an important and too-often overlooked history for those who seek to understand cultural expression and for those who seek to understand movements for social justice. This is required reading."

—Eddie Torres, president and CEO, Grantmakers in the Arts

"A motivating read. Ken Grossinger's examination of the many mediums and methods artists, storytellers, organizers, museums, and funders have experimented with to engage the imaginations of an often disengaged public, and the resulting historical reference, inspires courage to a new generation of justice-oriented artists."

—Jose Antonio Vargas, founder, Define American

"Hiring an experienced community organizer was a transformative moment for us at the Queens Museum, as the organizer enabled us to engage fully in the life of our community. In *Art Works*, Ken Grossinger makes a strong case for the past success and future potential of partnerships between organizers and arts groups."

—Tom Finkelpearl, former director, Queens Museum, and former commissioner, New York City Department of Cultural Affairs

"I'm so excited about the possibilities this book creates—the possibility to infuse our movements with joy and meaning through art, and thus make them more effective and impactful; the possibility to reach millions of people beyond the choir, through art that moves and inspires; and the possibility to visualize a different future our movements seek to create. May every organizer be inspired to expand our 'repertoire of contention' through art."

—Saru Jayaraman, president, One Fair Wage, and director, Food Labor Research Center at University of California, Berkeley

"Ken Grossinger understands the vital chemistry that happens when artists and organizers join forces. We can't ignore these lessons and insights if we want real political change in our lifetime."

—Tabitha Jackson, former director, Sundance Film Festival

"This is the book I've been waiting for, a rare primer to guide how we integrate art and organizing in our work for justice."

—Si Kahn, artist, organizer, and author of *Creative Community Organizing: A Guide for Rabble-Rousers, Activists, and Quiet Lovers of Justice*

"Ken Grossinger invites readers to explore the symbiotic relationship between art and cultural organizing in creating lasting political change. Each chapter reflects upon the past, present, and future of cultural organizing to suggest best practices moving forward. This book is essential reading for understanding how art can help foster the solidarity and connection sometimes missing from social movements."

—Dorian Warren, president, Community Change

"Our movement for freedom, justice, and dignity needs to reflect cultural roots. In *Art Works*, Ken Grossinger makes the powerful case for fusing art and organizing strategies. This is a terrific book. I'm giving it to many friends and savoring its message."

—Heather Booth, founder, Midwest Academy training center

"Ken Grossinger chronicles the combined power of artists and activists across history and how these collaborations have advanced social movements. I applaud Ken for bringing this important history to life. The Art for Justice Fund is grateful to be cited as an example of this significant tradition."

—Agnes Gund, founder and board chair, Art for Justice Fund

"Anyone who's organizing and working for environmental justice should read this book! *Art Works* demonstrates how art can elevate our educational and organizing work, while extending our reach beyond the choir."

—Lois Gibbs, founder, Center for Health, Environment and Justice

"Whether it's music, visual arts, theater, or beyond, human connection is central to making this world a fair and just place. Ken Grossinger not only illuminates this critical point, he invites us to sing a new future by calling on all parts of ourselves. A must-read for civil and human rights activists who aim to break through the noise."

—Maya Wiley, president and CEO,
Leadership Conference on Civil and Human Rights

"I have always known that the sounds and rhythms of music course through our movements for justice in America. But Ken Grossinger reveals the deeper connections between art and social change. *Art Works* gets at the heart of matter—it is essential reading for all justice-seekers."

—Michael Eric Dyson, bestselling author of *Tears We Cannot Stop*

"Focusing on stories of artists and organizers collaborating over a wide range of movements in *Art Works*, Ken Grossinger establishes the key principle for success when using art for social change: the affect of the arts and the effect of activism work better when working together."

—Stephen Duncombe, co-founder, Center for Artistic Activism

ART WORKS

How Organizers and Artists Are Creating a Better World Together

Ken Grossinger

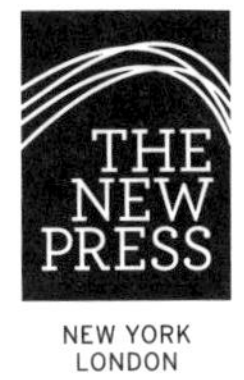

NEW YORK
LONDON

Published in the United States by The New Press, New York, 2023
Distributed by Two Rivers Distribution

ISBN 978-1-62097-672-2 (hc)
ISBN 978-1-62097-800-9 (ebook)
CIP data is available

The New Press publishes books that promote and enrich public discussion and understanding of the issues vital to our democracy and to a more equitable world. These books are made possible by the enthusiasm of our readers; the support of a committed group of donors, large and small; the collaboration of our many partners in the independent media and the not-for-profit sector; booksellers, who often hand-sell New Press books; librarians; and above all by our authors.

www.thenewpress.com

Book design and composition by Bookbright Media
This book was set in Minion and Nosta

Image credits for the Amplifier posters:
Top row from left: Kate DeCiccio + Amplifier for 826national.org, Kate DeCiccio + Amplifier for oxfamamerica.org, Alex Albadree + Amplifier for wearehome.us, Nina Yagual + Amplifier for yellowhouseart.org, Nina Yagual + Amplifier for yellowhouseart .org, Shepard Fairey + Amplifier for #DreamActNow.
Middle row from left: Jared Yazzie + Amplifier, Jess X Snow + Amplifier for womensmarch .com, Jess X Snow + Amplifier for womensmarch.com, Ernesto Yerena + Amplifier for womensmarch.com, Misha Zadeh + Amplifier for womensmarch.com, Rue Oliver + Amplifier.
Bottom row from left: Rommy Torrico + Amplifier for keepfamiliestogether.org, Rommy Torrico + Amplifier for opportunityagenda.org, Molly Crabapple + Amplifier for nomuslimbanever.com, Camila Rosa + Amplifier for gijtr.org, Camila Rosa + Amplifier for gijtr.org, Unapologetic Street Series + Amplifier for womensmarch.com

Printed in the United States of America

10 9 8 7 6 5 4 3 2 1

For Micheline

CONTENTS

INTRODUCTION

An upsurge of new alliances, fusing politics and culture, is altering the world of social activism.

Organizers have long contested for power through unions and community organizations that have the infrastructure to support political mobilization. Periodically, their work is boosted by protest movements that exert pressure on politicians and the corporations that wield political power. But even though popular mobilizations can generate legislative change, these policy shifts are often unsustainable. Depending on who's in power, politicians are apt to undo legislative reforms and concessions when power changes hands. The political pendulum keeps swinging, but a shift in public attitudes can make the gains harder to undo.

Many artist-activists who work without a political infrastructure are increasingly focused on changing how the United States and other nations respond to injustice. They are building what has recently been called "narrative power": taking control of the stories that shape how we think about history, culture, people, and places.

These artist-activists tap popular culture to tell important truths. They've played pivotal roles in virtually all movements for a more just and equitable society, from the photographers who exposed the brutality of white supremacy in the South, to needleworkers who, drawing on craft traditions, pieced together the AIDS quilt, one of the largest public art installations in America. Street and digital art in the form of projections, poetry, music, and visual images reached millions via social media, propelling activism in the Black Lives Matter movement. Music provided anthems for all these struggles.

Because politics and culture are inextricably linked, organizers and artist-activists are more likely to achieve lasting change in the body politic by working together. That sounds obvious, but until recently—as the field of cultural organizing started to develop beyond the work of the individual artist and as the organizing community has begun to open itself to new forms of collaboration—many activists and organizers had been selecting one path or the other. Many others are now merging their approaches to challenging power.

As *Art Works* documents, the strategic value of linking culture and politics with other social and economic forces is powerful. The following pages dive deeply into historical and contemporary movements during which labor and community organizers worked hand in glove with artist-activists and show how their joint work contributed to or restrained their progress.

Art Works features organizers who brought artists to their strategy tables to contribute their ideas beyond their art and artists who deployed their artwork in the service of social movements. The book explores the challenges of these collaborations and the extent to which organizations and artists have developed practices that enable or stymie their capacity to work together.

Art Works also examines two types of institutions—foundations and museums—to discuss how they are shaping viewpoints and whether they are supporting or disrupting strategies for change.

Each chapter draws on strategies that movement leaders, whether organizers or artists, have adopted to work together to advance social justice. In the real world, insurgent movements for change and issue-oriented campaigns work when they disrupt societal norms;

that happens when political action and culture penetrate popular perceptions.

A new wave of organizers and artists who are joining forces in movements for social change is rising. The opportunity to ride this wave gives us all hope for the future.

ART WORKS

1

"Freedom Is a Constant Struggle"

Art of the Civil Rights and Black Lives Matter Movements

They buried us but they didn't know we were seeds.[1]

The freedom songs of the civil rights movement bolstered activists' courage to protest for racial justice. While subjected to beatings and arrest for registering Black voters and for participating in nonviolent civil disobedience, activists sang to strengthen their resolve and overcome their fears. Wyatt Tee Walker, a director of the faith-based civil rights organization Southern Christian Leadership Conference (SCLC), said of "We Shall Overcome":

> One cannot describe the vitality and emotion this one song evokes across the Southland. I have heard it sung in great mass meetings with a thousand voices singing as one; I've heard a half-dozen sing it softly behind the bars of the Hinds County prison in Mississippi; I've heard old women singing it on the way to work in Albany, Georgia; I've heard the students singing it as they were being dragged away to jail. It generates power that is indescribable.[2]

"Freedom Is a Constant Struggle" is the title of a song written by Roberta Slavitt that became one of the anthems of the Southern civil rights movement.

Since the 1960s, it has been common practice for civil rights leaders to intentionally embrace music and other forms of art in tandem with their organizing strategy. In collaboration with organizers, artists breathed creative life into the movement and helped expose the nation and the world to the brutal violence white supremacists employed to subjugate African Americans seeking the franchise. Art in all its forms—from visual art, including photography and film, to poetry, music, theater, and more—was not just an interlude but a contributor to politics, helping to shape the worldview and culture of those within and on the sidelines of the civil rights movement.

Yet historians, and even the organizers and artists themselves, rarely focus on the importance of these collaborations. Instead, they choose to focus on individual works of art that give expression to social justice, but they omit the strategic value of linking art and organizing. This book examines and contrasts the impact of various collaborative practices as they have played out in social movements and campaigns. Within the civil rights and Black Lives Matter movements, these collaborations have differed in form, but they have all been essential.

In the civil rights movement, many creatives and organizers often worked together at the strategy tables. They combined the power of art and the political muscle of community organizations and popular protests to pressure the government and other institutions to change policies. They developed ideas and strategies in partnership with each other.

Many of these artists saw little separation between their art and their politics. Bernice Johnson Reagon, the founder of Sweet Honey in the Rock, said,

> As an activist in the Civil Rights Movement, I learned about the relationship between organizing for change and being a cultural artist. Most of us who became

> known during that time as singers or song leaders, saw ourselves as organizers. I saw again and again the connections between being an effective leader and a cultural artist.[3]

Two of several civil rights organizations that intentionally fostered collaboration between artists and organizers are the Student Nonviolent Coordinating Committee (SNCC) and El Teatro Campesino, a theatrical collaboration between the United Farm Workers (UFW) and artists that tells the story of migrant workers and their fight with agribusiness for fair wages and better working conditions. Movement leaders, including SNCC's Julian Bond, based primarily in the Southern civil rights movement, and the UFW's Cesar Chavez, based on the west coast, traveled the nation to promote civil and economic rights.

In some ways, these organizations created a blueprint that informs how artists and organizers today might, and sometimes do, work effectively together.

Reagon, a lead vocalist in the Freedom Singers, also served as a founding staff member of SNCC. Her husband Cordell Reagon and other SNCC leaders founded the Freedom Singers to raise money for the movement and to increase its national visibility. Their singing strengthened community bonds and inspired activists elsewhere throughout the South. Danny Lyon, staff photographer for SNCC, tells the story of fifteen-year-old Bettie Mae Fikes, who led a high school freedom chorus in a movement church in Selma, Alabama:

> The church was packed and steaming. Outside in the dark the police were waiting. No one was sure they could leave the church. . . . The clapping was like thunder as Betty Mae's [*sic*] great voice broke out high above the others. "This Little Light of Mine, oh I'm going to let it shine."

> Then she called out the names of their tormentors, "Go tell Al Lingo, I'm going to let it shine" and the church roared. "Go tell Jim Clark, I'm going to let it shine." Lingo was the notorious head of the Alabama Highway Patrol who favored electric cattle prods. Clark was Sheriff of Dallas County.[4]

Fikes, sometimes called the "Voice of Selma," became a SNCC student organizer and member of the Freedom Singers. As a teen, she was jailed for marching in a civil rights protest in 1963, and in 1965 she participated in the infamous Bloody Sunday march across Selma's Edmund Pettus Bridge, where white state troopers laid in wait to attack the marchers with nightsticks, cracking open the skull of then twenty-five-year-old activist John Lewis.[5]

Songs with deep roots in gospel music and the Black church were a vital part of SNCC's community organizing. SNCC organizer Courtland Cox said these songs "helped thaw some of the fear that locals had about the movement."[6]

It went both ways. Churches and community and labor organizations embraced artists, and artist-activists helped drive organizing. No artist in the civil rights movement was more prominent than Jamaican American singer and actor Harry Belafonte, who worked as a strategist, using his performing talents along with his leadership skills to help plan the civil rights movement. When referring to using his talents to advance racial justice, he would say, "I am not an artist who became an activist. I am an activist who became an artist."[7]

Storytelling was at the core of Belafonte's craft—both in his music and in his films, such as *Odds Against Tomorrow* (1959), which casts light on tense race relations, and *Beat Street* (1984), which is among the first films to showcase the culture of hip-hop and graffiti artists. His daughter Gina Belafonte, activist, filmmaker, and producer, would say he created content specifically to engage people from other walks of life. He used his films and songs of liberation, "his entire artistic platform, to educate, motivate and activate folks to [make] change."[8] In his memoir, Belafonte writes that "my days were jammed, my evenings too, in constant balancing between art and activism, tipped toward the latter."[9]

A confidant and adviser to Dr. Martin Luther King Jr., Belafonte was one of the lead organizers of the historic 1963 March on Washington, and he helped bankroll civil rights initiatives and organizations, including the Congress of Racial Equality (CORE) freedom rides in 1961, SNCC's 1964 Mississippi Freedom Summer, and Dr. King's SCLC.[10]

Belafonte called on fellow artists to draw attention to racial injustice, and they responded, using their craft and celebrity to promote civil rights. Marlon Brando joined the Freedom Rides, marched for civil rights, helped fund the SCLC and the NAACP, and took acting roles in such films as *Sayonara* (1957), in which Brando's character falls in love with a Japanese dancer and "deals squarely" with racism.[11] Comedian and civil rights activist Dick Gregory used satire with white audiences in the United States and abroad to shape public opinion and attack racial injustice. Belafonte even got actor and former NRA president Charlton Heston to support the 1964 Civil Rights Act, before Heston moved to the political right. Many civil rights leaders worked hand in hand with artists who, like Belafonte, contributed to strategic discussions and supported civil rights workers.

If It Hadn't Been for Music, the Civil Rights Movement Would Have Been Like a Bird Without Wings

Music was an ever-present force in organizing.[12] The powerful voices of singers Mahalia Jackson, Aretha Franklin, Peter, Paul and Mary, Joan Baez, and others sang out against bigotry and racist violence.

But it was not just "Negro spirituals" and freedom songs. Activists sang the blues, taking up a tradition that began with enslaved men and women working in plantation fields and with prison laborers whom Southern states used to replace enslaved laborers. Nina Simone periodically collaborated with civil rights leaders. Her "Mississippi Goddam" (1964) lyrics still ring out:

Hound dogs on my trail
School children sitting in jail
Black cat cross my path
I think every day's gonna be my last[13]

Jazz also played a role. In the early stages of the civil rights movement, Billie Holiday's 1939 recording of "Strange Fruit" was a shattering call for justice in the face of lynching:

Southern trees
Bearing a strange fruit
Blood on the leaves
And blood at the roots

Black bodies
Swinging in the southern breeze
Strange fruit hangin'
From the poplar trees[14]

Rutgers University Institute of Jazz Studies archivist Tad Hershorn said, "It did really leave both the singer and audience no place to hide."[15] Ahmet Ertegun, co-founder of Atlantic Records, called it a "declaration of war . . . the beginning of the civil rights movement."[16] Bernice Johnson Reagon said about jazz,

> This music had no words. But it had power, intensity and movement under various degrees of pressure; it had vocal texture and color. I could feel that the music knew how it felt to be Black and Angry. Black and Down, Black and Loved, Black and Fighting.[17]

These ideas were reflected in the challenging sounds of bassist Charles Mingus, saxophonists Coleman Hawkins and Archie Shepp, drummer Max Roach, and pianist Thelonious Monk. Drummer Art Blakey wrote "The Freedom Rider," a seven-and-a-half-minute jazz drum solo, three weeks after the 1961 Freedom Rides. John Coltrane's sax cried out "Alabama," a dirge responding to the death of the girls who died in the 1963 Birmingham church bombing.

Folk musicians Pete Seeger, Theodore Bikel, and Bob Dylan, among many others, performed at voter registration rallies in the cotton fields of Greenwood, Mississippi, and other venues. Dylan's fleeting but important role in the civil rights movement was reflected in his tribute to assassinated civil rights activist Medgar Evers. Dylan's "Only a Pawn in Their Game" was first performed in Mississippi and was later released in 1964 on his *The Times They Are a-Changin'* album. In an interview with Nat Hentoff for the *New Yorker*, Dylan said about SNCC that it was the "only organization I feel a part of spiritually."[18]

Seeger and Bikel performed such songs as "Keep Your Eyes on the Prize."

Paul and Silas bound in jail
Had no money for to go their bail
Keep your eyes on the prize, hold on

Paul and Silas thought they was lost

Dungeon shook and the chains come off
Keep your eyes on the prize, hold on[19]

Seeger and other white singer-songwriters, including Harry Chapin, Joan Baez, and Peter, Paul and Mary, became organizers of a different type. They collaborated with African American movement leaders and, like Belafonte, recruited other artists to join the fight. They embedded their work within the Black-led strategies of the civil rights movement. And they built on the radical tradition of labor organizations like the Industrial Workers of the World, commonly referred to as the Wobblies, a union that worked in the early 1900s with artists to produce and perform musical events explicitly to promote social change.

Musicians like Dylan, Simone, and Holiday kept their primary focus on their art while supporting civil rights protest and initiatives, leaving the more interactive strategy and planning to movement leaders and organizers. Each played distinctive and important roles.

Through these intentional collaborations, musicians and their songs touched the passions of the entire nation and helped drive attention to and broaden engagement with the civil rights movement. Activist, photographer, and author Bruce Hartford said, "The songs spread our message, bonded us together, elevated our courage, shielded us from hate, forged our discipline, protected us from danger, and it was the songs that kept us sane."[20]

Building SNCC's Campaign

In some ways, SNCC was a model for collaboration among artists and organizers who worked jointly on strategy, at demonstrations and in the halls of Congress. From its founding, SNCC absorbed a steady stream of practicing artist volunteers eager to work for civil rights, and these partnerships went beyond those well-known collaborations with musicians. SNCC integrated field operation with key arts programs that included a photography department, an independent press, and a theater company. SNCC's art programs also included creating essential comic books to teach politics in communities of color, using "the idiom and folk expressions of the South."[21]

In fact, SNCC's first staffer, Jane Stembridge, was a young poet, and amateur artist Jennifer Lawson, a young civil rights activist originally from Fairfield, Alabama, joined the SNCC staff at age twenty. Lawson illustrated the SNCC comic books and played an important role in reproducing the Black Panther image on signs and billboards, helping it to become a ubiquitous symbol of the SNCC-affiliated Lowndes County (Alabama) Freedom Organization (LCFO).

The panther imagery was a direct response to the Alabama Democratic Party's symbol, a white rooster, surrounded by the words "White Supremacy for the Right." Lawson recalls LCFO chair and civil rights activist John Hulett responding to the rooster symbol by saying, "We need a mean black cat to run that rooster out of this county."[22] Lawson said if she could get lumber and paint, she could create billboards, reproduce the LCFO's Black Panther image and voting message, and spread it around town. A 1966 billboard read "Pull the lever for the Black Panther and go on home!" Lawson said,

> To promote the elections in Lowndes in May (primary) and November (general election) 1966, we created billboards to place on main roads in Lowndes. Black landowners allowed us to use their land to erect these notices, which were both to encourage people to vote (pull the lever for the Black Panther) and for safety (go home).[23]

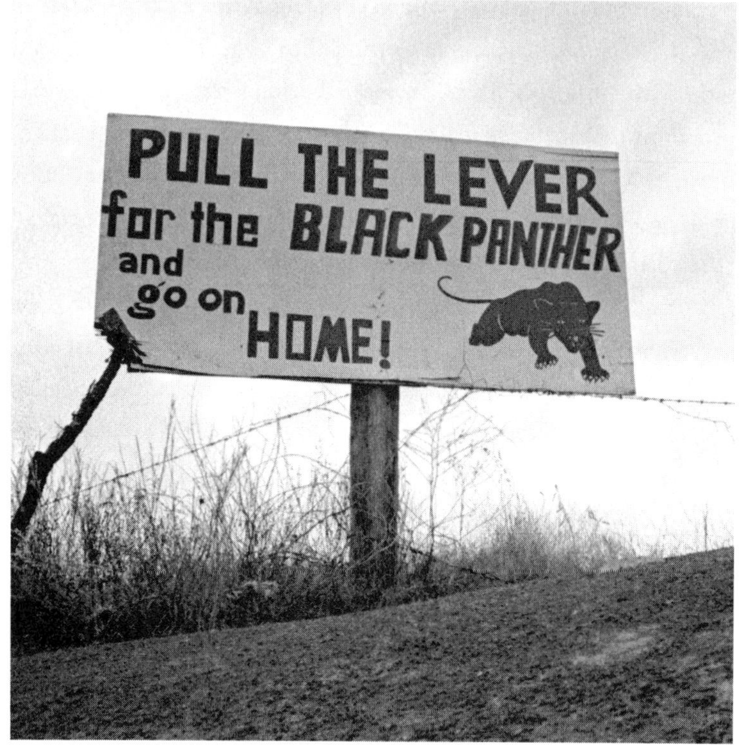

Photo by Jim Peppler, November 1966. Courtesy of Alabama Department of Archives and History.

Shaping Public Opinion

In addition to musicians, painters, and illustrators, photographers also embedded themselves in the civil rights movement and exposed segregationist and police brutality to the nation and to the world. In 1962, SNCC director James Forman hired twenty-year-old Danny Lyon, a self-taught photographer from New York, whose two-year stint with SNCC captured visual images of the Southern civil rights movement in real time, creating a legacy archive.

Lyon tells one of many stories of how his early photographs influenced events during the fight for civil rights. In 1963, in Americus,

Georgia, police detained thirty-three African American teenage girls for protesting racial segregation. The girls were imprisoned for up to forty-five days without charges, locked in the Leesburg Stockade and forced to use "a common toilet that quickly stopped up" and to sleep on concrete floors without mattresses or blankets.[24] Lyon recounts how "they had all but been forgotten by the world" until he captured images of the girls through the "glass of barred windows," which were subsequently delivered by SNCC to *Jet* magazine (and other news outlets) for publication. Pennsylvania senator Harrison Williams entered the images into the congressional record. They were also given to U.S. attorney general Robert Kennedy. With national attention focused on the images of the young girls, imprisoned for exercising their right to protest and detained without due process, a call for action and the release of the young girls was swift.[25]

Shortly thereafter, in 1964, SNCC budgeted $34,055—equivalent to $323,192 in 2022—to create a photography department that included photographers Maria Varela, Tamio Wakayama, Bob Fletcher, Clifford Vaughs, Geoffrey Clark, Herbert Randall, Doug Harris, and Julius Lester, who in 1967 became head of the SNCC photo department.[26]

SNCC photographers provided "uncontestable visual information about the movement."[27] Their work was used in SNCC organizing materials, exhibitions, and brochures and for fundraising. In the early 1960s, photographer Bob Adelman volunteered to serve both SNCC and CORE, capturing portraits of civil rights leaders and images of demonstrations, sit-ins, and police brutality. Like Lyon, Adelman's photography skills added another dimension of visibility and accessibility to SNCC's strategic approach to social change.

Ralph Ellison, author of the influential book *Invisible Man*, said Adelman's work "moved beyond the familiar cliches of most documentary photography into that rare sphere where technical ability

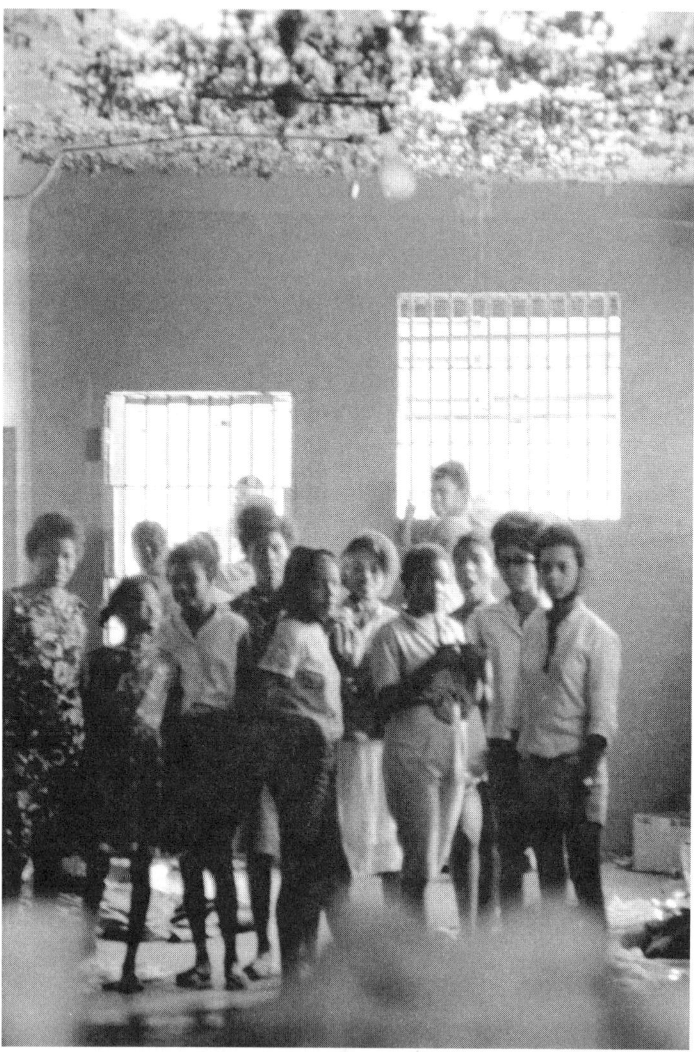

Teenage girls were detained for up to forty-five days for protesting racial segregation in Americus, Georgia. Held in the Leesburg Stockade, they had no beds and no working sanitary facilities. August 1963. USA. Leesburg, Georgia. Photo © Danny Lyon/Magnum Photos.

and social vision combine to create a work of art."[28] It was exactly what James Forman had in mind: a collaboration model, where art and organizing merged for impact.

Storytelling in the Battle of Ideas

Civil rights organizers also embraced theater as a tool to foster dialogue, recruit activists, and add comic relief to sometimes dire circumstances.

In 1963, SNCC field directors John O'Neal and Doris Derby and student leader Gilbert Moses created the Free Southern Theater (FST). Supported by established popular artists Langston Hughes, Ossie Davis, and Ruby Dee, among others, and with resources from the Ford and Rockefeller Foundations, FST performed in rural areas and small Southern towns. O'Neal argued that in "telling stories, and working through metaphor, rather than argument, people come to shared understanding more quickly."[29] In other words, evoking emotion was a powerful way to win the battle of ideas. Two of their best-known productions were *When the Opportunity Scratches, Itch It*, which "comments on power dynamics among different social classes in the African American community," and *Where Is the Blood of Your Fathers?*, which uses historical text from Frederick Douglass and others to explore the life of slavery.[30]

In 1965, UFW organizers, including the young Cesar Chavez, joined forces with Luis Valdez (considered the father of Chicano theater) to form El Teatro Campesino (the Farm Workers' Theater). Growing out of the grape boycott for decent pay and working conditions in central California, this performance collective and would-be political operation contested for power with agribusiness and the far right. In reflecting on its history, UFW co-founder Delores Huerta said their primary aims were to "keep the spirits up of the workers who were already on strike and to try and reach people who the growers would bring in as strike breakers. . . . It was a very powerful organizing tool—as powerful as the picket line."[31] The theater company also enabled workers to speak out about such issues as immigration

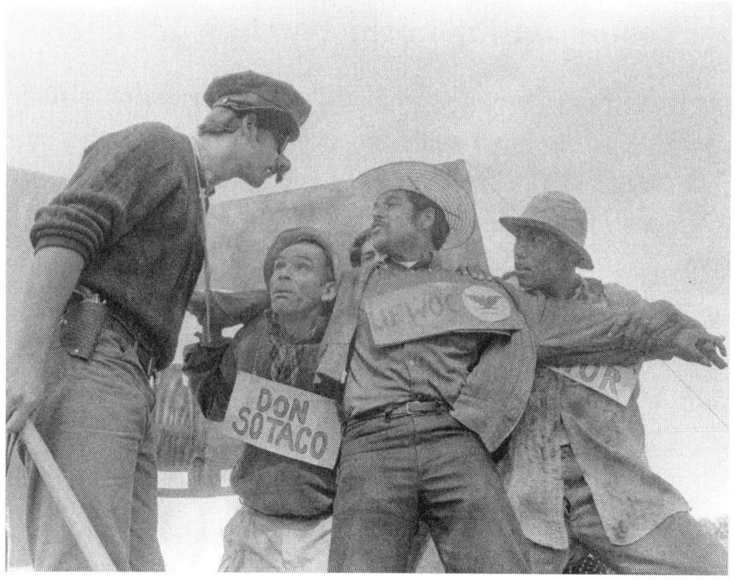

El Teatro Campesino's skit helped buoy the spirit of workers on the grape boycott picket lines. Photo by John Kouns, 1966. Courtesy of the Tom and Ethel Bradley Center, California State University, Northridge.

and their own working conditions. It was among the first important joint labor and cultural initiatives of the twentieth century.

Labor had undertaken a handful of cultural projects in an earlier era. One union, the International Ladies' Garment Workers' Union (ILGWU), a predecessor of UNITE HERE, used theater between 1937 and 1940 to boost the public's opinion of organized labor through a Broadway production called *Pins and Needles*.[32] With 1,108 performances over three years, this Broadway hit, written and performed by union members—sewing machine workers, cutters, and basters—became the longest-running Broadway show of its time.[33] Its opening number, "Sing Me a Song with Social Significance," followed by "It's Better with a Union Man," generated solidarity among audience members, while the play offered a glimpse of how theater can be used to build public interest in the lives of working families.

Like the garment workers in *Pins and Needles*, farmworkers in El Teatro Campesino acted in skits and in their own voice spoke to the issues permeating UFW struggles. El Teatro said, "It is not necessary to be an actor, since the most important experience in this theater is obtained through the picket line."[34] It set a precedent for theater companies today, such as the Los Angeles Poverty Department, a theater and activist group made up of people living in downtown Los Angeles's Skid Row, who work in tandem with the ACLU and other organizations advocating for unhoused people.

Unlike *Pins and Needles*, El Teatro performed in public spaces, on the backs of pickup trucks and on the roadside by fields where farmworkers picked grapes and other produce. In support of the struggle, musician-activists Woody Guthrie ("This Land Is Your Land") and Pete Seeger, whose life and music were dedicated to organizing for justice, performed in migrant worker camps to create opportunities among the workers for gathering in community and solidarity. Guthrie's "Pastures of Plenty" (1941) and "Deportee" (1948) highlighted the plight of immigrants. "Deportee," a protest song translated into Spanish by Baldemar Velasquez, the founder of the Farm Labor Organizing Committee, helped popularize the 1960s farmworkers' struggle.

These songs and El Teatro's performances, including tours in Mexico and six tours to Europe, garnered national and international attention. In 1969, the California-based El Teatro received a Los Angeles drama critics award and an Obie, the annual award established by the *Village Voice* to recognize excellence in off-Broadway and off-off-Broadway theater, for using its art to demonstrate the "politics of survival." In 1981, following other successes, El Teatro introduced *Corridos*, the story of a young man who becomes indebted to a smuggler while trying to cross the border, only to wind up working for poor wages in terrible conditions.[35] The production played to sold-out houses, was critically acclaimed, and received eleven Bay Area awards, including best musical.

El Teatro had real impact at two levels. Farmworkers found inspiration for activism and sometimes comic relief from their backbreaking work. For non-farmworkers and the nation at large, El Teatro's work dramatized the largely unknown plight of exploited immigrants and the conditions in which they lived. By increasing public attention, the troupe raised substantial funds for farmworkers and their organizing campaigns and challenged the way political and corporate leaders portrayed these workers. University of Maryland professor Randy Ontiveros said,

> [El Teatro] turned the dominant perspective [about immigrants] on its head. Instead of scapegoating immigrants for the economic crisis created by a free market system, El Teatro presented them as protagonists in a dramatic confrontation between workers and corporations.[36]

And, of course, its impact could also be seen in the backlash. Agribusiness attacked UFW members and their leaders, while members of the John Birch Society, a far-right organization dedicated to opposing civil rights gains, took gun shots at the troupe.[37] But the theater persisted. In 1999 it opened a multimedia digital center to reach new audiences and thereafter linked its work with communities of color. It remains a model of how artists and unions can effectively use theater to build the power of a local and national movement by, for, and benefiting farmworkers.

Artists Organize Among Themselves

Former beatnik Amiri Baraka founded the Black Arts Movement (BAM) in 1965, ushering in a new era of cultural conflict. Primarily based in the northern states, BAM concentrated on organizing artists rather than on rooting their work inside a civil rights organization. The lines between these artists and movement leaders were porous, and the nature of their collaborations varied dramatically.

BAM blended activism with poetry, theater, and music to lift up Black revolutionary culture and Black pride. Following the spirit of the Harlem Renaissance of the 1920s, when artists like Langston Hughes challenged American racism, BAM affirmed a Black aesthetic. Nationally and internationally known poets Nikki Giovanni and Sonia Sanchez, musician and spoken word artist Gil Scott-Heron, and visual artists Betye Saar and Faith Ringgold were among those who gave BAM a defining presence. Indeed, Giovanni believes "BAM gave birth to the Black Power Movement."[38]

While SNCC, El Teatro Campesino and the UFW, and the union-based performance of the ILGWU acknowledged and cultivated the role of music, photography, and theater within the lifeblood of their organizations, BAM took a different tack, focusing on the value and power of visual and literary artists, poets, and other artists who organized themselves to supplement the work of labor and civil rights organizations.

The Poetry Foundation describes BAM as the sister to the Black Power movement, its cultural arm:

> Despite its brief official existence, the movement created enduring institutions dedicated to promoting the work of Black artists, such as Chicago's Third World Press and Detroit's Broadside Press, as well as community theaters.

> It also created space for the Black artists who came afterward, especially rappers, slam poets, and those who explicitly draw on the movement's legacy. Ishmael Reed, a sometimes opponent of the Black Arts Movement, still noted its importance in a 1995 interview: "I think what Black Arts did was inspire a whole lot of Black people to write. Moreover, there would be no multiculturalism movement without Black Arts. Latinos, Asian Americans, and others all say they began writing as a result of the example of the 1960s. Blacks gave the example that you don't have to assimilate. You could do your own thing, get into your own background, your own history, your own tradition and your own culture."[39]

Cultural Organizing Spurs Black Lives Matter

The struggle for racial justice has taken a turn in the decade spanning 2012 to 2023. "Conventional" art-centered organizing—street and pavement murals, public art installations, films, quilts, and billboards—was augmented by a growing number of artists and organizers who took advantage of new advances in technology and used the internet, digital projections, and social media to mediate relationships with their audience. By coupling communication, art, and organizing strategies on the ground and digitally, these activists reached millions more people in the United States and abroad, who joined the growing mobilization against racial bias and police brutality.

Speaking to the value of connecting art and organizing, in March 2012, rapper Jasiri X released "Song for Trayvon," in response to the February 26, 2012, killing of Trayvon Martin, an unarmed seventeen-year-old who was walking home from the convenience store with a Snapple and a bag of Skittles. "Song for Trayvon" was featured heavily on the internet and social media and major radio stations. Millions of audience members have listened to Jasiri X and other hip-hop artists perform songs about George Zimmerman and Trayvon, including Jay-Z ("Try That Shit with a Grown Man"), Vince Staples ("Hands Up"), Usher ("Chains"), Kendrick Lamar ("The Blacker the Berry"), and Lady Gaga ("Angel Down"). Individually and together these songs helped shape a national response to injustice, particularly in the African American community.

In 2013, in response to the acquittal of George Zimmerman, who had shot and killed Trayvon Martin, Oakland-based domestic worker organizer and activist Alicia Garza wrote a "Love letter to Black people" in a public Facebook post:

> Black people, I love you. I love us. Our lives matter, Black Lives Matter.[40]

Collaborator and artist-organizer Patrisse Cullors added a hashtag, and social media strategist Opal Tometi fueled the growing digital presence that initially powered #BlackLivesMatter. Reflecting the escalating demands for racial justice, organizations like the Movement for Black Lives—an alliance of over a hundred Black-led organizations—emerged and helped build out a popular movement of activists. Together with state and local organizers and unaffiliated grassroots activists who used social media as a tool to express their rage, concern, and calls for justice, they helped to create the largest multiracial movement in a half century.

Like all social movements, the political priorities of Black Lives Matter activists ranged widely, from antiracist organizing, to ending mass incarceration and the restoration of felons' voting rights, to elevating the fight for gender, economic, and environmental justice.

Sustained protest heightened the movement for racial justice. BLM's national visibility grew, particularly after police killed Eric Garner on July 17, 2014, in Staten Island and when less than one month later, on August 9, 2014, police shot and killed eighteen-year-old Michael Brown in Ferguson, Missouri. Garza said, "Hashtags don't build movements. People do."[41] Local organizers in Missouri coordinated door-to-door canvassing and house meetings in Ferguson and St. Louis County, while nationally, activists, including Patrisse Cullors and Darnell Moore, organized the Black Lives Matter Freedom Rides to recruit activists to Missouri, creating momentum for the entire movement.[42]

Like organizers, artists can respond quickly and strategically—often in very public ways—when they are touched by events such as the ongoing assaults on the Black community. In this case, their work immediately filled the streets, airwaves, and social media. Hundreds of musicians stepped up, taking to YouTube and other streaming platforms. Digital organizing through song and video played an essential role in support of movement strategy. For instance, Tom Morello used his song "Marching on Ferguson" to raise funds to help pay the legal fees of Ferguson protesters, by offering viewers a free download of the song and asking for voluntary contributions. Morello wrote,

A nation at half-mast
Figured I'd get the last laugh
carving up the golden calf
with a blowtorch and gasmask
I'm marching on Ferguson
I'm marching tonight.[43]

Released in 2015, Rhiannon Giddens's "Cry No More" starts out with Giddens drumming a slow and steady beat on a frame drum, as if she were a warrior gearing up for a fight. Her haunting song was created in the aftermath of the 2015 mass shooting in which an acknowledged white supremacist murdered nine African American worshippers at the Emanuel AME Church in South Carolina. The song is a passionate and defiant call for unity and action.[44] With only her frame drum and voice, Giddens uses a call-and-response song style, with a church choir refrain "I," and then "We Can't Cry No More." A few of its stanzas follow (without the refrains):

First they stole our bodies/Then they stole our sons
Then they stole our gods/ And gave us new ones
And then came generations/That helped to build this land
The bedrock of the nation/Was laid with these brown hands
And then they stole our solace and then they stole our peace
with countless acts of malice and hatred without cease
Our legacy is mighty/We can't carry this alone
You have to help us fight it/And together we'll be home
(We can't cry no more)[45]

In June 2020, activists once again poured into the streets, joining together in ever-larger numbers to protest the gruesome killing of George Floyd in Minneapolis, Minnesota. The artists among them used film, music, social media postings, quilts, and art exhibitions to capture and propel the protest movement in Minnesota and across the nation. In demonstration after demonstration, organizers invoked the words Floyd gasped more than twenty times to police, "I can't breathe," as it became a cultural symbol of resistance and a political call to arms. A co-founder of the Weather Underground, Bill Ayers, commented, "'I Can't Breathe' somehow combines the pandemic with the endemic, the endemic of racism and white supremacy, with the pandemic that we're all living through."[46]

As protests spread, community artists created street murals in tribute to Floyd, his family, and the thousands of Black and Brown people terrorized and murdered by the police. Artists painted on plywood used by retail stores to board up broken windows, on brick walls, on residential homes, on streets, and on school buildings. A trio of artists, Cadex Herrera, Xena Goldman, and Greta McLain (with help from others), created among the first of hundreds of murals of George Floyd. Twenty feet wide and six feet high,

> the [trio's] mural has a light blue background, giving way to a sunflower with Floyd's face and upper body in the head of the flower; with the names of others, including Sandra Bland, Tamir Rice, Philando Castile, Breonna Taylor, Michael Brown, Jamar Clark, and more, surrounding him. Large, block orange letters read "George Floyd" with outlines of people in each letter, raising their fists to the sky.[47]

The mural, painted close to where Floyd died, created a space to mourn—a public community remembrance for Floyd and the many Black and Brown victims of police terror. *See Plate 1.* Local, national, and international media stories took this mural as their backdrop, and artists immediately replicated it in their own styles across the United States and around the world, including in Australia, Ireland, Kenya, Syria, Canada, Belgium, and Palestine. The Floyd mural became an iconic image of the early twenty-first century. A symbol of protest. A tribute. A way to heal.

Murals have the power to project the pain of key moments in history and to become sites of gathering, mourning, and inspiration.

Artists created "Say Their Name" murals that rang out at demonstrations and jolted people around the world. The act of painting a name in public and saying it aloud shattered the silence that surrounded much of the violence against people of color.

In Oakland, California, artist Shara Shimabukuro painted a Floyd mural featuring George's daughter's saying "Daddy Changed the World." In Washington, DC, Ginevra Frank's mural *Tree of Life* inscribed the names of those murdered by police on the tree's leaves. New York City muralist Matthew Mazur painted an image of Angela Davis on Wooster Street in SOHO saying "I'm no longer accepting the things I cannot change. I'm changing the things I cannot accept." Other images invoked 1960s figures, like Gil Scott-Heron and his song "The Revolution Will (Not) Be Televised." And still others included the slogans "Black Girls Deserve Better," "Justice for Breonna," "Be the Change/Go Vote," "Demilitarize the Police," and "Do You Understand Yet?" The murals added visual power and spark to the ongoing protest movement.[48]

Artists created downloadable posters for activists to use in street actions: *This Stops Right Now* by Eso Tolson, *Love Has No Color* by Jean Carlos Garcia, *There Comes a Time When Silence Is Betrayal* by Edinah.[49] These expressions of rage and calls to action helped dramatically alter perceptions of race relations and state-sanctioned violence against Black people by drawing connections between those who have power and privilege and those who have neither.

Building off the Floyd murals, billboards and public art installations helped create a climate for change. Hank Willis Thomas created *All Power to the People*, a twenty-eight-foot-tall, seven-thousand-pound African hair pick, installed—initially—near the birthplace of Martin Luther King Jr. For Freedoms, an artist-led organization founded by Thomas and Eric Gottesman, used billboards designed to awaken the nation and to get potential voters to vote. They collaborated with art institutions, such as museums and galleries, as well as with schools and community organizations. In support of grassroots organizing, the For Freedoms Awakening 2020 Billboard Project engaged dozens of artists and communities to create politically potent billboards in local venues. These billboards were also used as a basis for community dialogue about the growing movement for racial justice.

Artist Sofía Gallisá Muriente uses a pink roadside billboard in Puerto Rico to ask us to *Imagine Freedom* (Imaginos La Libertad). Montpelier, Vermont, artist Mutale Nkonde uses black letters on a red background to ask *Have You Mailed In Your Ballot?* To honor Breonna Taylor, Chicago mayor Lori Lightfoot saw to the creation of thirty-two electronic billboards asking you to *#SayHerName*.

Quilters picked up their needles. South Carolina quilter Peggie Hartwell created an *Ode to George Floyd* that depicts Floyd staring dazedly toward a barely discernible image of his mother and the words "I can't breathe." Hundreds of other narrative quilts told Floyd's story.

As artists have so often done, they also raised money to fund wider civic engagement. In a project called Artists Band Together, Barbara Kruger, Jenny Holzer, Luchita Hurtado, and twelve other artists designed and sold bandanas to support community organizing and voter engagement. They collaborated with organizations such as Mijente, a political action hub for digital and grassroots Latinx and Chicanx organizing and movement building. Other fund recipients include RISE, which organizes students, and Woke Vote, which focuses on registering and mobilizing Black voters. Co-curator and activist Nora Halpern said the bandanas project "is rooted in the history of bandanas as symbols of unity. From the Abolition movement to Rosie the Riveter, bandanas have been wearable markers of alliance and action."[50]

Social media and music videos became almost universal broadcasting platforms. Music artists Usher and Nas teamed up to create the multiplatform "Chains," about lives lost due to racial profiling. Donald "Childish Gambino" Glover's music video "This Is America" was viewed internationally 839 million times.[51]

Throughout the racial justice protests, particularly following Ferguson and escalating in the aftermath of Floyd's death, poets and performers intensified the political moment. Spoken word poet and LGBTQ activist Staceyann Chin created stage performances that went viral.[52] Films—notably *Whose Streets?* (2017), about the Ferguson uprising; *Baltimore Rising* (2017), following the death of Freddie Gray; *Selma* (2014) and *13th* (2016), which made Ava Duvernay a household name—raised the issues. *Fruitvale Station* (2013), which offers a searing look into police brutality, and *Just Mercy* (2019), which illuminates the injustices of mass incarceration and death row, based on the book by the same title written by prominent public interest lawyer Bryan Stevenson, added to the voices, visibility, and justification for the activists' political demands. In June 2020, comedian Dave Chappelle's performance *8:46*, about the murder of George Floyd, was released on Netflix's YouTube channel Netflix Is a Joke and viewed by more than 32 million people.[53]

Innovations in technology gave artists new organizing tools. They created work designed for digital formats—music videos, GIFs, and memes—that supported digital organizing. Twitter, and particularly Black Twitter, amplified voices of protest. Activists also made powerful use of digital projections on the streets, including projecting a seventy-foot-high image of George Floyd's face on the Robert E. Lee statue in Richmond, Virginia.[54] Artists were also able to emblazon slogans and images on buildings and other statues in public spaces, to give visibility to high-profile messages without violating laws governing property rights and the "defacing" of public institutions.

The explosion of art and community organizing and the use of social media that permeated the second decade of the twenty-first century were spectacular, and reminiscent of how civil rights movement activists integrated art with their fight for racial justice, but supplemented by digital organizing. As *New York Times* writer Charles Blow commented,

> A generation of young people and young artists found their voices and used them, creating an arts movement that sits in the canon alongside the Black Arts Movement of the 1960's and 70's and the Harlem Renaissance.[55]

Three months before the Trump-Biden presidential contest, Michael Brown, Freddie Gray, Eric Garner, Tamir Rice, Sandra Bland, Breonna Taylor, and George Floyd had become household names. Meanwhile, Donald Trump used the police and displays of military power to maintain his white-power base and drive a false law-and-order narrative. He called out the military and Department of Homeland Security (DHS) personnel to squash nonviolent protests. Trump's insertion of DHS troops in Portland, Oregon, to suppress growing protest fueled popular indignation and uprisings on the streets of Seattle, Los Angeles, and elsewhere. *See Plate 5.* Former president Barack Obama condemned the Trump administration for turning federal and military police into his personal army. The United Nations Human Rights Committee spoke out, saying, "The international treaty governing civil and political rights requires states to allow peaceful demonstrations, not to block or disrupt them without a compelling reason."[56]

In addition to murals going up on walls and in digital spaces, Washington, DC, mayor Muriel Bowser engaged city workers and activists to paint BLACK LIVES MATTER in large yellow letters covering two city blocks across from the White House, an area the

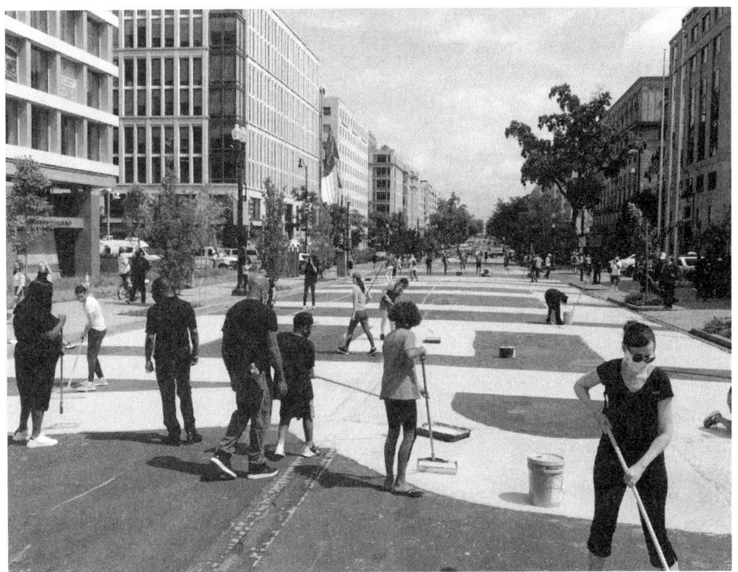

Pavement murals spread throughout the nation during the Black Lives Matter movement. Photo by Charles Green III, 2020.

mayor designated as Black Lives Matter Plaza. Some DC activists took umbrage, arguing it was a "yellow wash" of their demands, and immediately created a second pavement mural with DEFUND THE POLICE. Notwithstanding the dustup, new BLM pavement murals began to surface throughout the country, appearing in dozens of cities across twenty-eight states, including Texas, Colorado, Alabama, California, Louisiana, and North Carolina.

With a visibility akin to street murals, artists in Portland, Oregon, documented the "Wall of Moms," in which participants used their status as mothers to protect demonstrators and journalists from beatings by Trump's army. Putting themselves on the front lines between police and protesters, these women followed a long global tradition, seen in "Mothers of the Disappeared" in Argentina and the "Black Sash" in South Africa during the apartheid regime. These Portland moms, clad in yellow or white, were soon followed by a

"Wall of Dads" and a "Wall of Vets" (which formed after the beating navy veteran Chris David received at the hands of the federal police). Then came the "Wall of Artists," who documented it all.

Tactically, organizers and artists waged a clear and unambiguous assault on the historical narratives used to perpetuate racism. They prioritized turning these narratives about race, mass incarceration, and police brutality on their head. Few approaches exemplified this better than their approach to monuments.

The use of memorials, statues, plaques, and historical markers to glorify and perpetuate white supremacy is not new. Many monuments erected after the Civil War as part of a backlash to Reconstruction became freighted symbols of resistance to civil rights. These public commemorations of revisionist history are contested ground. In the South, civil rights activists have long fought to remove statues of white male "heroes" and monuments that glorify oppression and distort how we see the world.[57] Racial justice activists saw the value and tactical advantage in targeting monuments. They created a powerful local focus for street protest. After a seventy-foot monument to the Confederacy was taken down at the University of Louisville, in Kentucky, and after New Orleans mayor Mitch Landrieu removed four Confederate statues, the focus on monuments spread like wildfire. These monuments became what James W. Loewen described as "flashpoints for protest," just as local organizers and artists had envisioned. Activists toppled statues in Alabama, Massachusetts, Florida, Georgia, Indiana, Kentucky, Pennsylvania, Minnesota, Tennessee, Virginia, and elsewhere.[58] Progressive federal, state, and local elected officials who opposed the use of racist symbols soon joined protesters in condemning memorials to enslavers who symbolically guarded white privilege. In Congress, Speaker Nancy Pelosi passed HR 7573 to remove the statues and busts of Confederate leaders that sat in the Capitol. White support for the removal of Confederate memorials and statues climbed from 39 percent in 2017 to 52 percent in 2020.[59]

Artists also began to subvert the imagery of historic sculptures. In 2019, portrait artist Kehinde Wiley, well known for his portrait of President Barack Obama, on display in the National Portrait Gallery, created a striking sixteen-foot-high monument he called *Rumors of War*. It sits in Richmond, Virginia, along Arthur Ashe Boulevard, just a little more than an hour's drive west of Charlottesville, where the now infamous Unite the Right rally marched two years earlier. Wiley designed *Rumors of War* in the tradition of earlier artists who portrayed Confederate generals sitting on horseback as symbols of white domination. Hewn from stone or cast in bronze, these monuments signified power and permanence. Their sheer height enabled the generals to metaphorically look down on viewers, while forcing viewers to look up passively from a position of inferiority.

With an artistic twist, Wiley replaced the white Confederate leaders with a young, muscular Black horseman sporting dreadlocks and sneakers. He thus both reimagined how leaders might look and mocked the Confederate generals by imagining an African American in an equal position of power.

Visual artist Matt Hunter created a somewhat similar display in a different medium in the mural *A New Monument for a New Future*, featuring Breonna Taylor riding a powerful-looking horse, her arms pumped up, right hand in a fist.

Wiley's memorial is described by the Virginia Museum of Fine Arts as "directly engaging the national conversation around monuments and their role in perpetuating incomplete histories and inequality."[60] South African contemporary art curator Tumelo Mosaka described Wiley's narrative shift in a short essay:

> Wiley creates a tension with canonical art history, and its neglect of Black subjects that is not simply oppositional. Instead, his portrait symbolically reassigns value to the sitter, asking the viewer to recall remarkable Black leaders such as Toussaint L'Ouverture, Martin Luther King and Nelson Mandela, whose images appear far less frequently, if at all, in histories of art.[61]

Artwork in the form of music, film, poetry, photography, painting, sculpture, and other genres has always helped shape narratives about racial justice. This is one reason why it is so critical for art and antiracist organizing to be interconnected. Mobilizations, community organizing, and conventional issue campaigns are limited in impact when they don't produce a shift in culture. Too often the fights that community, labor, and political leaders wage are confined to winning or losing one public policy issue or another, without addressing the attitudes and values that give rise to these issues. The campaign to topple monuments is ongoing. But artists, pols, and activists have begun to reimagine the future by tearing down old monuments and conceiving new monuments to people and events the nation can properly be proud of.

The different forms of collaboration in the social movements discussed here reflect varying approaches to social change. Artists such as those who work with For Freedoms organize among themselves and link their work to community organizations to help drive movements for change. Other artists and organizers work hand in glove with each other, as did SNCC and El Teatro Campesino. The Movement for Black Lives and grassroots artist-activists and digital gurus continue to advance campaigns for racial justice.

The cumulative impact of this artwork matters greatly. Art can reinforce a culture of protest and its often oppositional nature can spur a rethinking of the issues and circumstances it enshrines. The vast array of art in all of its forms interacts with, builds on, and responds to demands for social change. While social movements can result in important policy changes, organizing alone is unlikely to produce long-term change if we are unable to touch the heart and soul of our communities and shift the narratives that maintain the status quo. Cultural organizing does that.

2

"Singing for Our Lives"

Music and Anthems for Our Planet

Song defines the culture within which protest movements occur. As an emotional medium with the power to open a crack in mindsets and conventional assumptions, music influences popular ideas that intersect with organizing. Protest movements give rise to song, just as songs help spur protest.

This chapter dives deeply into the role of music in just a few of the many environmental justice struggles at the dawn of the twenty-first century. It explores the sometimes catalytic impact of collaborations among and between musician-activists and organizers. These alliances include musicians who use their craft and celebrity to partner with organizers and activists and campaigns led by community and labor organizations that use the power of music to carry a message.

Musicians United to Protect Bristol Bay is a landmark illustration of collaboration, a story that brings together schoolchildren, artists, and activists. It's a story of third graders in an Indigenous Alaska salmon-fishing community who came up with a campaign message. And it is also a story of artists and activists who forged an international movement to hold off a high-powered environmental threat. Music was a small but important part of the fight.

Between 2002 and 2007, a Canadian multinational corporation,

Holly Near wrote the song "Singing for Our Lives" following the assassination of San Francisco City County supervisor and gay rights activist Harvey Milk. The song became an anthem for the LGBTQ movement.

Northern Dynasty Minerals (NDM), invested $180 million to develop what it called the Pebble Project, a plan to dig the world's largest copper and gold open-pit mine near the salmon-spawning headwaters of Alaska's Bristol Bay region.[1] It would stretch more than a mile in length, a mile wide, and 1,750 feet deep.[2] The proposal to build what came to be called the Pebble Mine immediately created warring political factions pitting the powerful Alaska fishing and extractive mining industries against each other. Caught in between were Indigenous communities and the jobs and livelihoods of thousands, with potentially devastating effects on the environment and tribal ways of life.

Though Indigenous people represent 15.6 percent of Alaska's population, over 65 percent of the families living in the Bristol Bay region are Indigenous and identify as Yupik Eskimo, Alutiiq, and Athabaskan.[3] These First Peoples of the region are among the 229 tribes indigenous in Alaska, most of whom still live in close intrinsic connection to the land and surrounding waters.[4] The Indigenous people of the Bristol Bay region have lived in villages along the rivers for over four thousand years, with 80 percent of their consumed protein coming directly from fishing, hunting, and gathering on the land and waters.[5] According to Yupik fisherwoman Alannah Hurley, who serves as the executive director of United Tribes of Bristol Bay, a tribal consortium working to protect traditional ways of life in southwest Alaska, "It is impossible for Pebble to mitigate the devastation this mine will have on our Native cultures."[6]

The environmental toll on the land, water, fish, and wildlife and the loss of employment within the fishing industry if Pebble is built would be wrenching. Some fifteen thousand full-time and part-time workers in the Bristol Bay watershed generate an estimated $2.2 billion of economic value, working in jobs ranging from boat crews to marine supply store staff, warehouse packers, shippers, salespeople, and maintenance personnel for refrigeration and other mechanical devices.[7] The mine would tear at the economic and social core of communities and potentially destroy 3,500 acres of wetland and 81 miles of salmon streams. The pristine Bristol Bay waterways have always been the largest single source of sockeye salmon in the world, consistently supplying more than half of the world's sockeye salmon.[8] In 2022, the Alaska Department of Game and Fish estimated 75 million fish would flow through Bristol Bay.[9]

Increasing the risk of economic and cultural devastation, the seismically active Castle Mountain Fault is situated 18 miles from the proposed Pebble Mine, according to the company. Two U.S. Geological Survey analyses of the land suggest it may be within 5 miles. But the Alaska-Aleutian megathrust is just 125 miles from the proposed mining site. In 1964, it triggered a 9.2 earthquake, the second largest earthquake in recorded history, shaking the ground for four minutes and thirty-two seconds.[10] The fault line rupture extended for 600 miles and caused twenty-one tsunamis—destroying communities, businesses, and basic infrastructure and killing over 130 people.

According to the Pebble Mine plan, a seventy-story-tall earthen dam would hold up to 10.2 billion tons of toxic waste from the mine tailings.[11] Bristol Bay, one of the great remaining wild places in the world, for Indigenous peoples, traditions, cultures, and languages and for the richest remaining sockeye salmon fisheries in the world, could be marred or destroyed forever.

Twenty years after NDM obtained the rights to the mine, it remains unbuilt. A powerful Indigenous-led movement that includes Alaska Native corporations, many Alaska citizens, artists, national and international environmental organizations, legal advocates, public officials, and organizations representing people who fish for subsistence, for sport, and for business has so far stopped the mine in its tracks.

The fight to prevent the mine began almost as soon as NDM announced its intention to develop it. In addition to strong Indigenous-led organizing, some Alaskans who opposed the plans for the mine were musicians. Dan Strickland is a porch-picking folk music lover who had fished in Alaska for decades. Former Alaska state senator Suzanne Little, who now works to support Alaska public land and river conservation for the Pew Charitable Trusts, is also a longtime songwriter and bluegrass band member. Lifelong Bristol Bay resident Bryce Edgmon, the first Alaska Native to be elected speaker of the Alaska House of Representatives and who had fished Bristol Bay for over twenty years, is a politically influential singer-songwriter from the Curyung tribe railing against the mine.

As groups rallied against the pressure from NDM, these artists realized that the campaign had no soundtrack, no anthem, no central rallying song around which they could galvanize public support. Strickland and Little persuaded North Carolina–based folk musician Si Kahn to volunteer for the campaign, to get to know the Bristol Bay community and their fight, and importantly, to write them a campaign theme song. Kahn is both an internationally known recording artist and a longtime organizer in the civil rights and labor movements who began his organizing career in 1965 with the Student Nonviolent Coordinating Committee (SNCC). As part of his learning tour, Strickland took Kahn to an elementary school class in Dillingham, the main town in Bristol Bay, where they met with a dozen third-grade Indigenous students known as the "Rebels to the Pebble." Kahn offered to be their musical messenger if the children would tell him what message to deliver. With guidance from the students, Kahn created the song "Abundance."

When you hear the word "subsistence"
Do you think of someone poor with an outstretched hand

To us it means abundance
Living off the richness of the land

We've been here ten thousand years
Along this river shore
If there's any justice left
We'll be here ten thousand more

The first salmon of the season
We always take and give to someone else
Any game we carry home
We feed others before ourselves

No power known can ever force me
From this ancient place that gave me birth
From the richness of the river
And the abundance of the earth[12]

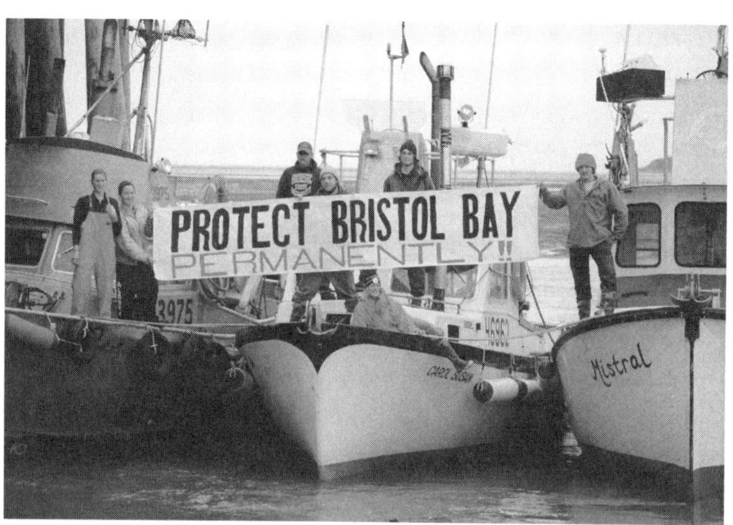

Cover image of Si Kahn's 2013 album Bristol Bay. *Photo © Lukas Strickland.*

The song, one of many Kahn wrote in his role as a "musical journalist" for the campaign, inspired his album *Bristol Bay* (2013), which also served as a fundraiser for Musicians United and which got significant airplay on English-language folk radio around the world. Kahn and Little preformed "Abundance," along with other songs the two of them had written, not only in Bristol Bay but at festivals and fundraisers, in communities and concerts, and on radio stations throughout Alaska, Canada, and the Lower 48.

In addition to working with Bristol Bay youth, Little, Strickland, and Kahn also helped build an organization to recruit activists and artists, raise funds, and spotlight the campaign to reach a national audience. They called their newly founded, loosely organized, and underfunded endeavor Musicians United to Protect Bristol Bay.

Musicians United was not just a musical adjunct; their work was driven primarily by campaign needs and strategic collaboration with allied organizations to mobilize opposition to the mine, and they worked to harness the power of performing musicians and their audiences. In its broad efforts to stop Northern Dynasty, organizers embraced an effective arts-centered approach to build, develop, and strengthen their campaign for justice. The value in this movement-building approach can best be considered by drawing a distinction among three different forms of collaborative practice between musicians and organizers. One obvious role musicians play is to perform at events—to inspire activists, raise money, build community, and fire up protests. These deliberate, yet intermittent, relationships between artists and organizers give broader exposure to issues and stir public interest and political action. Thirty-nine original songs protesting the Pebble Mine were submitted to the Musicians United 2017 songwriting competition and continue to be performed by musicians over the world. Musicians can help move a crowd, and organizers know it.

A second form of collaboration that may have more enduring impact happens when musicians and organizers work more consistently and closely with each other in various settings and phases of the campaign, and in doing so, each engages potentially new or different audiences. In this emergent form of collaborative practice, musicians, taking inspiration from pressing issues, may write and record music specifically to galvanize protest or change behavior, such as the song "Don't Throw It Away" (2019) by Grammy Award–winning blues musician Keb' Mo', which urges people to use reusables and to rethink the impact of single-use plastics.[13] His song is especially trumpeted by partner and collaborator Plastic Pollution Coalition, a global alliance of more than 1,200 organizations and businesses in more than seventy-five countries and with more than a hundred artist-ally supporters.

Musicians United took a third approach, embedding their work in an alliance that included tribal leaders, community organizers, lawyers, and members of the Bristol Bay fishing community and mutually sharing their ideas for campaign strategy. Musicians were not seen by organizers as "simply" performers with no other resources to offer, and organizers were not seen by musicians as disconnected from culture. This shared respect enabled Musicians United to embed their work in the overall campaign against Pebble Mine, much as the SNCC Freedom Singers were embedded in the civil rights movement.

For Strickland and Little, collaboration and trust included hosting evenings in their homes, where Kahn's songs were performed and "test-driven" before audiences of Pebble Mine opponents. When the feedback was "they need fixing," the songs were edited.[14] If, ultimately, the audience had not wanted a song to be heard publicly, it would have been scrapped. This iterative practice engaged both the artists and community and built trust in a shared vision for the music inside the campaign.

In addition to Kahn, other performing artists wrote and recorded songs for the campaign. Prominent artist and actor Tom Chapin included "Prayer for Bristol Bay" and "Ride Out Any Storm" in his 2015 album *70*. The same year, Tret Fure, president of Local 1000 of the American Federation of Musicians, AFL-CIO, recorded "The Fishermen of Bristol Bay" on her album *Rembrandt Afternoons*.

Perhaps the most widely recognized and respected musician to join Musicians United was the legendary Pete Seeger, who made a video in support of the campaign. Sitting in his log cabin home in Beacon, New York, in front of a world map that included Bristol Bay, which had hung on his wall for decades, Seeger said,

> Many people are pessimistic about the future of the human race, because doing what seems profitable in the short run, in the long run is destroying the earth. However, musicians all over, in many different places, are showing that their music can get people together to fight to save this earth and to save the human race.
>
> Si Kahn, down in the South, was contacted by the people way up in Bristol Bay, a place where a lot of the fish that we eat come from. And the whole bay is threatened now through the possibility of being wiped out by people who want to put a big copper mine there, an open-pit copper mine. And when they do that, Bristol Bay will be no more.
>
> So, whether you're a musician or not, I hope you'll get behind this battle to save this wonderful part of the world. I, Pete Seeger, am proud to be a member of

> Musicians United to Protect Bristol Bay. Hope you will be, too.[15]

Demonstrating their understanding of cultural influence, Musicians United expanded their partnerships with athletes in the lead-up to the annual Iditarod, a long-distance dogsled race between Anchorage and Nome, Alaska.[16] Because of their iconic status, Iditarod mushers, who ride and control dogsleds, receive international press attention and wide support throughout Alaska.

In 2014, musher Monica Zappa, a distant relative of musician Frank Zappa, and her team of huskies used the race as a vehicle to campaign against Pebble Mine. Supported by legendary Iditarod racer Tim Osmar, Zappa's sled and dogs were decked out in "No Pebble Mine" graphics, generating national media coverage along the route. To raise awareness and funds for the team's participation costs, Musicians United kicked off the race with a public concert that featured legendary Yupik musician and artist Aassanaaq "Ossie" Kairaiuak and the Acilquq traditional Yupik dancers.

Their creativity also flourished in concert at Salmonfest, a three-day summertime musical extravaganza held in Ninilchik, an old Russian Orthodox fishing village about five hours south of Anchorage. Salmonfest's director-producer is Jim Stearns, a thoughtful, direct-talking, get-to-the-point kind of guy who for ten years worked as the backstage manager of hospitality for the Grateful Dead. He previously founded the California-based High Sierra Music Festival and conceived of Salmonfest as a hybrid musical and political event that would garner support for the campaign against Pebble Mine.

The forty-acre concert area, with multiple stages, provides many venues for musicians, poets, and community leaders to speak out. At eight thousand attendees, Salmonfest is one of the largest gatherings of any kind in Alaska, second only to the annual state fair. Participants, clad in hiking and muck boots and prepared for changing weather, dance at the stages and move between amphitheaters and their campground. Frequently ten-, twenty-, and thirty-foot salmon replicas parade throughout the festival grounds. The original logo was a clenched fist holding a salmon.

In a sea of tents, tarps, and food vendors, the festival site also has a social action center—Salmon Causeway. Festival volunteers and bands playing on stage direct attendees to the center, where activist organizations like Musicians United distribute educational material, conduct voter registration, and recruit activists to the fight. The festival also raises money to donate to a wide swath of "grassroots Pebble Mine–fighting entities," including the United Tribes of Bristol Bay, InletKeeper, Kachemak Bay Conservation Society, Alaskans Know Climate Change, and Musicians United.[17]

Stearns holds the widely shared view that the mine battle will continue until the state government revokes the lease owned by Northern Dynasty. He notes, "There's a half-trillion dollars sitting underground, and the jackals are going to continue to circle until the last one of them is put to rest."[18]

During the Obama administration, in 2014, the EPA forestalled the mining operations by denying the mining companies permits to dig. But in 2017, within hours of a meeting between Trump-appointed EPA administrator Scott Pruitt and Tom Collier, then CEO of the Pebble Partnership that represented investors in the mining operation, the Trump-era EPA withdrew Obama's plan to protect the watershed of Bristol Bay, enabling the company to revive its permitting applications.[19]

Stearns understands the power of music both to cultivate and to nurture environmental activists and, equally as important, to reach people who do not know about the potential impact of the mine or who might support its development. People from all sides of the

Pebble Mine fight attend the festival to hear music and to party. In different years, Grammy Award–winning artists Emmylou Harris, Ani DiFranco, Lucinda Williams, the Indigo Girls, and Brandi Carlile have performed. Carlile commented,

> Alaskans of many different political persuasions are coming together to protest the building of the pebble mine in Bristol Bay that is threatening to decimate the largest salmon concentration in North America and along with it, the livelihood and legacy of many many proud Alaskans. The community against the pebble mine is coming together and their voice is being heard. As a long time salmon fisherwoman and a lover of Alaska, I was proud to stand with you all last night and add my voice and play you some rock and roll![20]

It was not a coincidence that most of the many headliners were women. Drawing on his experience in the music industry, Stearns also wanted to use the festival to redress what he called the "misogynistic and patriarchal" character of the music business, so he deliberately made women headliners a festival trademark.[21]

Musicians United Building on a Legacy

Using concert venues to build public support for change has long proved effective. More than a half century ago, in 1966, folk icon Pete Seeger founded the Clearwater Festival to clean up the Hudson River.[22] In 1969, he went on to start the Hudson River Sloop Clearwater, an organization dedicated to sustaining the festival activities throughout the year. Continuing today, the Clearwater operation has drawn old and current performers, including Odetta, Tish Hinojosa, Taj Mahal, Dar Williams, and Steve Earle.[23]

Almost four decades later, in 2004, former Grateful Dead guitarist Bob Weir joined forces with bassist Marc Brownstein, of the jam band the Disco Biscuits, and then sportswriter Andy Bernstein to create an organization called HeadCount, originally dedicated to using concerts to register people to vote. They would soon be joined by the Dave Matthews Band and other popular entertainers. From the stage, band members directed concert attendees to what they called Participation Row, where, like at the Salmon Causeway, they could register to vote and receive material on climate change and other issues. Their voter registration initiatives consistently resulted in higher turnout rates during subsequent elections—sometimes 10–12 percentage points higher than the turnout rate in the general public.[24]

As the battle against Pebble Mine continued, Alaska leaders asked Musicians United to extend their reach. "We've got Alaska covered. Don't worry about Alaska."[25] Told they could best serve the Pebble Mine fight by broadening the campaign in the Lower 48, Musicians United recruited artists who lived outside of Alaska, who came to compose 90 percent of the organization. This expansion supplemented the work of advocate organizations in the Lower 48 to pressure the EPA, congressional legislators, and the Army Corps of Engineers, who oversee mining permits, to prevent the mine from opening. Artists performed at annual music events, such as the Folk Alliance International, showcased their work at the International Bluegrass Music Association, and held press conferences at which they performed and spoke on the need to stop the proposed mine. Moreover, increased visibility allowed Musicians United to cultivate donors from outside Alaska, adding another source of financial support for their campaign. Dozens of musicians augmented the work of the national "big green" organizations opposing the mine.

It's easy for musicians to spread the word in song and spirit because musicians have loyal followers, and many musicians are trusted messengers. With more than twenty albums to his name, Kahn observes that "people develop close emotional bonds with the artists they love, even if they've never met them. Even if they don't know them personally."[26]

Beyond performing at concerts, musicians manage mailing lists and social media contacts with thousands or even millions of fans. Their fan bases far exceed the number of activists reached through the mailing lists of environmental organizations. Musicians sometimes function like organizers in that they make targeted appeals to their base, and to the extent they are organized to do so, they can share jointly in the strategic work of building a broader alliance.

In 2016, while Kahn was in Ottawa recruiting Canadian musicians for Musicians United, longtime friend and social justice activist Sari Tudiver introduced him to MiningWatch Canada, an advocacy and research organization that supports the sovereign rights and authority of Indigenous communities. Based on this connection, and with a grant achieved by Musicians United, the organization contracted with MiningWatch Canada to investigate the corporate investors who bought the land lease for the proposed Pebble Mine site. MiningWatch alleged that Northern Dynasty created thirteen related corporations that would allow it to avoid potential liability in the event of an earthquake, a break in the earthen dam, or other disasters.[27]

This investigative report dovetailed with the Natural Resources Defense Council (NRDC) campaign against the mine, targeting potential and current corporate investors. The NRDC pressed their case with top mining officials, bought stock in these companies, and attended shareholder meetings with community leaders and elected officials. Simultaneously, they identified and presented potential investors with a compelling analysis of the risks associated with their future investments in the mine. At different times, international corporations, including Rio Tinto, Mitsubishi, and Anglo America, and other potential new investors eventually opted out of the project.[28]

The Homestretch

Musicians connected to issue campaigns often build on or generate work from others within the art community. Perhaps no celebrity artist is more closely associated with the environmental movement than Robert Redford. He cut his teeth on environmental activism in the early 1970s, during the fights over public lands, clean air, and clean water. Lending his image and name to the Pebble Mine fight further exposed the risks inherent in the mining operation. These risks appeared to weigh especially heavily on Cynthia Carroll, then CEO of Anglo American, during her forty-five-minute presentation to her company shareholders in London in April 2012 on the company's performance over the previous year. NRDC senior attorney Joel Reynolds recalled how Carroll devoted almost twenty minutes of her presentation to the Pebble Project, in particular to Redford's engagement against it, accusing Redford and the NRDC of "distributing misinformation" and "making outlandish claims" in their effort to activate public opposition. She described to the shareholders how even her own mother had received a letter from Redford, causing her mother to ask Cynthia what she was doing that made him so upset.[29]

Performing artists with long histories in environmental justice fights, like Redford, have an authenticity that appeals to millions of their fans. Their track records add credence and weight to their message. It was not one song or album, one exhibition or advertisement that had critical impact, but the integration of the arts with the organizing done by the larger alliance of tribal leaders and community organizations that deepened and broadened the Pebble Mine campaign's public reach.

Immediately following the election of Joe Biden, on November 25, 2020, the Army Corps of Engineers denied the Northern Dynasty mining permit, stating that it did not comply with the Clean Water Act guidelines and would not serve the public interest—a decision NDM is likely to appeal. And then in 2022, the EPA said it would "protect waters in Alaska that are home to one of the world's biggest salmon spawning grounds."[30] As of this writing, the company has yet to respond, though some think the EPA's action could be the fatal blow that shuts down the proposed mine for good.

The work of Musicians United is an important illustration of how organizing—specifically environmental politics—and music can be fused. Jackson Browne said, "Art is like a banner, it's like a flag to rally around. It's a thing that gives you a feeling of unity and strength and optimism. . . . It's about a feeling of hope."[31] Songs have the capacity to stir the imagination and spur other artists and individuals to come together and speak out.

The success of Musicians United pivoted around their relationship with the campaign team. Musicians and organizers solicited input from Indigenous leaders, community organizations, and activists alike. They sat at the strategy tables on equal footing, exchanging their ideas and creative impulses in decision-making.

Developing a shared respect enabled Musicians United to seamlessly weave in and out of different aspects of the operation. Artists were centered in the campaign and partnered in the strategy. They sang, danced, and nourished the fight, forging a sense of solidarity, building a larger community, and bringing some oft undervalued fun to the campaign.

It's a difficult model to emulate, as musicians can't always take time away from writing, recording, and performing to embed their work in social movements. When they do, their participation adds texture to these campaigns and gives new voice to activists' demands. It's a lesson for organizers to learn. Musicians have a loyal following, a strategic contact list, and fundraising prowess. Like other activists, musicians have much to contribute.

The cultural and political insights of musicians and their ability to, in the words of Flacks and Rosenthal, "help to verbalize our collective beliefs" are frequently overlooked, notwithstanding their ability to put their fingers on the pulse of a community and give expression to their grievances and aspirations in ways that talking points do not.[32] Rapper Jasiri X comments that "often times I lament that movement art is always last" in terms of movement priorities.[33]

Collaboration Challenges

Historically, many national environmental organizations have been slow to adopt art as a pathway to reach a broader audience and deepen their campaigns. Author, activist, and founder of 350.org Bill McKibben discusses the origins of the problem this way:

> The environmental community in some measure grew out of science. That was where much of its original work came from. And so, it's always done a far better job of appealing to whichever hemisphere of the brain it is that likes bar graphs and pie charts, which is truly important. [But] winning the argument isn't enough because our decisions and things are not all based in reason and data. So figuring out how to work with the visceral side of the human brain is just as important.[34]

At the inception of the modern-day environmental movement in the late 1960s and early 1970s, organizers, scientists, and artists worked mostly in their own silos.

Referring to the first Earth Day on April 22, 1970, organizer Denis Hayes, now head of the Bullitt Foundation, which prioritizes green grants, said, "We did not know much about art. It seemed a little bit frivolous compared to the hard driving social and political goals."[35]

To illustrate the depth of that sentiment, Hayes revealed that visual artist Robert Rauschenberg had gifted fifty signed lithographs to the organizers in support of the Earth Day events. Hayes explained, "We didn't know if Rauschenberg was the next Picasso or just kind of a nothing burger," and eventually put the lithographs out in recycling. Hayes's sentiments, which have changed since the 1970s, are noteworthy because even fifty years later this orientation to art—that it lies at the margins of the environmental movement—persists among some organizers.

Even with well-known musicians releasing extraordinarily popular and environmentally themed songs—such as Joni Mitchell's "Big Yellow Taxi" (1970), Marvin Gaye's "Mercy, Mercy Me" (1971), and Jackson Browne's hit "Before the Deluge" (1974)—musicians and organizers who spoke out were on parallel but separate tracks, with rare exceptions.

Fast forward fifty years and we find this changing. Today, local environmental justice organizations are stepping up their embrace of artists, and artists are more centered on supporting the climate change movement. In 2005, McKibben wrote his now well-known essay in *Grist*, "What the Warming World Needs Now Is Art, Sweet Art," in which he sought out the cultural components of the environmental movement. He asked, "Where are the books? The poems? The plays? The goddamn operas?"[36] Four years later, in a companion piece for *Grist*, he began to chronicle the shift in practice and the rise of contributions from different art genres in relation to the climate change movement. Artists are now producing a torrent of new work in response to the increase in severity and risks of climate change, and they, along with environmental organizers, are demonstrating a heightened interest in collaboration.

At roughly the same time as Musicians United was investing in the fight over the Pebble Mine, the Hip Hop Caucus was having a vastly different experience with their role in the 2014 People's Climate March.

Founded by Rev. Lennox Yearwood Jr. in 2004 to engage vulnerable communities in climate change and, more broadly, environmental justice fights, the Hip Hop Caucus links politics and the arts to reach communities of color. They teach artists about environmental justice, connect them to community organizations, produce albums and music videos, and, beginning recently, stage stand-up comedy routines and use film to engage new audiences. The guiding principle is that when art and organizing are coupled, their chance of having a broader impact is greater than when they work alone. On face value, this might seem obvious. But in bringing art and organizing together, Liz Havstad, executive director of the Hip Hop Caucus, and Rev. Yearwood are, like many organizational leaders, having to navigate sometimes difficult terrain.[37]

In the run-up to the 2014 People's Climate March and the Paris Agreement in 2015, the Hip Hop Caucus produced what Havstad said may have been one of the only, if not the only, albums of climate change songs.[38] The album, entitled *HOME (Heal Our Mother Earth)*, featured renowned rapper Common, R & B singer-songwriters Ne-Yo and Raheem DeVaughn, and pop singers Antonique Smith and Candice Glover, among others.

Historically, musicians have produced environmentally themed concerts and albums to raise funds, such as the MUSE (Musicians United for Safe Energy) concerts and album in 1979 and the 2013 Earth Day celebration and Call to Action album. The Hip Hop Caucus's goal differed. They designed the *HOME* album as a soundtrack for the environmental movement, to mobilize public support for U.S. climate action, including President Obama's Clean Power Plan to curtail carbon pollution from the nation's power plants and public opposition to the Keystone XL Pipeline.[39] The EP (extended play) version of the album, which included a subset of the full LP (long play) version, was also used the same weekend of the People's Climate March in live performance in Washington, DC.

HOME caught the attention of many, in part because the Caucus negotiated a deal with iTunes (transitioned to Apple Music) to offer online access to the album. iTunes featured it alongside promotional adverts with other big-name artists and made a concerted effort to push it out to their subscribers. In the first week, listeners downloaded *HOME* 65,000 times. *HOME* reached audiences well beyond climate change activists. It was particularly resonant in communities of color.

The Hip Hop Caucus expected the organizations behind the People's Climate March to embrace the album in the way that it was intended to be used, as a tool for mobilization. Yet environmental organizations were ambivalent about how to use the album and what their call to action would include. Havstad said there was a "mismatch" between the coalition partners' desire to use it to promote specific policy changes and to solicit petition signatures and the entry point of the audience, who responded to art, not policy.[40] Cultural production was, once again, taking a back seat.

Rev. Yearwood argues that historically, the environmental movement has been strong on "suite activism," or policy and politics, but less interested in art and street activism. "Activism in the street needs a beat," he would say.[41] Additionally, the "Big Greens" have long maintained a white male–dominated leadership, and Yearwood believes art, and in this case hip-hop, was excluded from some of the climate march mobilization efforts because it did not reflect the primarily white culture of national environmental organizations.

Still, Havstad said the process for making the album was "transformative" for both the artists and the organizers involved. Most of the artists, including Common, had not written songs about climate change before. They were, in Havstad's words, "using their musical gifts to support a social movement."[42] Common's verse for "Trouble in the Water" was written following long discussions at the recording studio about the Clean Power Plan and the impact of pollution on communities of color. It was the same year Michigan governor Rick Snyder, a Republican, diverted the source of drinking water in Flint, Michigan, that contaminated the water supply with lead and other toxic chemicals. Subsequently, Common turned his recording of "Trouble in the Water" into a music video, a call to action that drew together his experience writing songs and working for racial justice with verse around environmental hazards, a crucial connection in building a broader base of activists.

For organizers, the collaboration was unique in that many of the white-led environmental organizations were now taking their lead from a Black-led initiative.[43] Many environmental organizations had no direct experience using hip-hop to engage community, nor were they accustomed to following the leadership of artists and relinquishing control over their output. To this extent, Havstad said the album served as a learning tool for organizers and artists, and as a shot at reaching new audiences with their message.

While the Hip Hop Caucus is not shy about critiquing the climate change movement and their collaboration, their role, nevertheless, in raising awareness and participation in the 2014 People's Climate March itself was extraordinarily successful. They galvanized public sentiment in support of the 2015 Paris Agreement and increased participation and visibility during demonstrations on the local, national, and international stages. They also cast light on the challenges in joining political and cultural work within an organizing framework, a key task ahead.

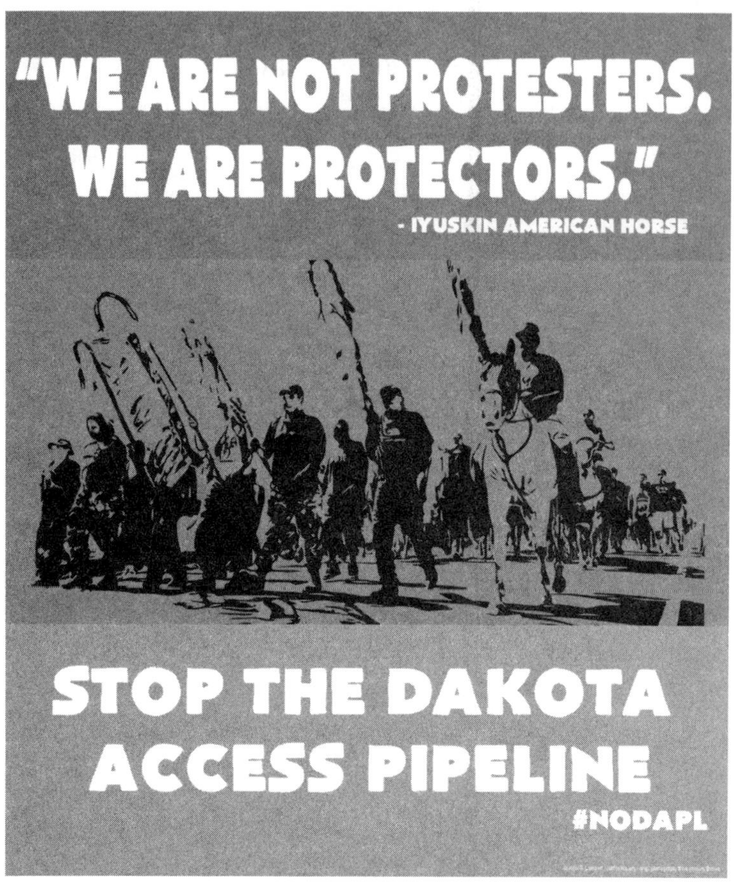

Poster art is now more prevalent in environmental justice fights. Targeting the Dakota Access Pipeline, this image was also screen printed as large patches by Nicolas Lampert and others at the Oceti Sakowin camp at Standing Rock in the fall of 2016. Courtesy of Nicolas Lampert.

Music in Service of Protest

In 2016, another key moment in the fight for climate justice garnered national attention when Indigenous and non-Indigenous artists took a stand against the Dakota Access Pipeline (DAPL). Running some 1,172 miles through the burial and sacred sites of the Standing Rock Indian Reservation in North and South Dakota and down to Illinois, the pipeline would carry an estimated 500,000 barrels of oil daily. Early on, the DAPL leaked 176,000 gallons of crude oil, immediately pointing up the threat it posed to the land, water, and lifestyle of the 8,200 families who lived on the Sioux reservation, and perhaps to the millions of people who lived downriver and rely on its water. The pipeline also posed substantial environmental risks to mammals, such as river otters, and racoons, and three hundred bird species, as well as to plants and trees. A major leak could cause irreparable damage to the reservation and harm the health and wellness of the Sioux community and lead to forced relocation.

Rising up to preserve and protect their way of life, Indigenous communities led the Standing Rock battle against the pipeline. Three hundred federally recognized tribes joined in protest. They created a temporary infrastructure for protection from the freezing weather and for providing activists with food and sustenance. They knew it would be a long haul.

As with Pebble Mine in Bristol Bay, musicians became part of the fightback. Through their music, hip-hop artists like Chance the Rapper and Vic Mensa amplified resistance to the pipeline. In 2016–17, the Hip Hop Caucus was invited to work with six-time Grammy Award–winning rapper Taboo, a member of the Black Eyed Peas band and the Shoshone Tribe. Taboo organized seven prominent Native hip-hop artists—called the Mag7 artists—to produce an album and music video entitled *Stand Up/Stand N Rock*.

Three million people viewed the video album on YouTube alone, not to mention on other social media platforms. It was nominated for an MTV Video Music Award, reaching 6.4 million people. Native artist Quese IMC called hip-hop "the deepest form of original spirit; it is a way to use our voices, words, and beats to carry us, so that we can carry the spirit of our message to the people."[44]

Several other performing artists supported the Indigenous-led organizing campaign. Neil Young created a music video entitled "Indian Giver," which served as another rallying cry. The first stanza set the stage:

There's a battle raging on the sacred land
Our brothers and sisters have to take a stand
Against us now for what we all been doing
On the sacred land there's a battle brewing[45]

Longtime activist-musicians, including Dave Matthews, Jackson Browne, and Bonnie Raitt (and Young), performed concerts in venues ranging from Fort Yates, North Dakota, close to the protest site, to media centers such as Washington, DC. They drew national attention to the pipeline fight, which until then the mainstream press had failed to cover in substantive ways. Raitt echoed activist frustrations:

> I'm proud to be standing in support of the courageous and dedicated water protectors at Standing Rock. This movement is growing by the day, yet the media isn't covering it nearly enough. . . . Our hope is that this concert will put pressure on the Obama administration to halt construction of the Dakota Access Pipeline until protection of sacred sites is ensured.[46]

These concerts also raised funds to support the tribal encampments, to weatherize their shelters, and to provide legal assistance to those many Indigenous leaders and activists who were arrested, detained, and brought into court by the North Dakota police.

The day before the *Stand Up/Stand N Rock* music video release, the Army Corps of Engineers stopped the pipeline, setting the Hip Hop

Caucus into overdrive to shift the message to one celebrating and honoring the "water protectors."

Immediately after taking office in 2017, President Trump signed an executive order to advance the DAPL, and it now falls to the Biden administration, awaiting the court's review of an environmental impact statement, to close it down. As in the Bristol Bay campaign, the swinging political pendulum spotlighted the need to strengthen organizations that sustain the fight.

Ultimately, the power of music to spur social change and to speak to and across generations of music enthusiasts clearly lies not just in its message but also in its ability to connect, inspire, console, reflect, and drive audience responses. Through song, musicians have created emotional connection in political moments and across time. In their book *Playing for Change*, Rosenthal and Flacks note that

> the popular song form has the unique ability to enter into the flow of time-driven events that dominate the mind of a listener . . . and to draw that listener into a space that exists outside of a time; a safe mental space from which entirely new approaches to society and personal living may be considered. . . . No other art form can do this as well.[47]

Collaborations between artists and organizers in grassroots movements and national campaigns take shape in different ways, from the spontaneous and changing rapid-response calls driven in the moment by political events, to the long, hard work of cultivating audiences and organizing infrastructure to support social change.

Knocking down the barriers to collaboration is key to making long-term shifts in policy, politics, and culture. Reconciling the longstanding and seemingly intractable issues of race- and class-related issues and the institutional and community arrangements that thwart collaboration is one task at hand. Just as trust develops between artists and their audiences and between organizers and their communities, trust can develop between organizers and artists. Each may have to step outside their comfort zone, but aided by the many artists who are also organizers and organizers who are also artists—as Musicians United, the Hip Hop Caucus, and Standing Rock protesters illustrate—doing so is well within reach.

3

Moving Images

The Power of Film in Political Mobilization

> *The world changes according to the way people see it, and if you alter even by a millimeter, the way . . . people look at reality, then you can change it.*
>
> —James Baldwin[1]

James Bridges's thriller *The China Syndrome* (1979), featuring Jane Fonda, Jack Lemmon, and Michael Douglas, brings viewers into a nuclear power plant on the verge of a meltdown. The story exposes the multiple risks associated with generating nuclear energy and raises public doubt as to whether the industry's inherent conflict of interest—between corporate profitability and the cost of safety precaution—can be reconciled.

The timing proved uncanny. The film thrust the risk of nuclear contamination and corporate corruption into public consciousness just as the government and private sector sought to build new nuclear power stations. It premiered nationally twelve days before the real-life partial meltdown of a reactor at Three Mile Island (TMI), a nuclear generating station in Pennsylvania.[2] Widely considered to be the most serious nuclear accident in U.S. history, the incident resulted in significant radiation leaks and was classified as "an accident with wider consequences," a five on the seven-point International Nuclear and Radiological Event Scale.

In a terrible twist of fate, TMI reinforced the film's warning about the hazards inherent in nuclear technology. *The China Syndrome* earned almost nine times its budget at the box office and four Oscar nominations at the fifty-second annual Academy Awards.[3]

The China Syndrome's wide exposure sparked public debate among nuclear experts and helped change individual ideas about nuclear energy.[4] On a more personal scale, Jane Fonda noted the film's effect on CNN founder Ted Turner, who told Fonda that the movie turned him against nuclear energy.[5]

Though not explicitly linked to on-the-ground organizing against the expansion of nuclear power plants and stockpiles, the film helped fan the flames of the antinuclear movement by providing activists with a cultural hook to organize the movie's millions of viewers. But were it not for the prophetic and coincidental timing of the film's release and the TMI meltdown, it is difficult to know what the film's impact would have been beyond its vast popular appeal and entertainment value.

Filmmakers and community organizers who strive to transform the political landscape don't depend on the element of chance. They believe narrative change alone is insufficient to change cultural norms, institutional practices, and policy. Marketing campaigns can effectively drive film into popular culture, but where does it go from there? Human rights documentary filmmaker Pamela Yates observes,

> What documentary films do best is to reach and unleash a wide variety of emotions. If at the end of the film you don't have a place to go with these emotions, then the emotional high is lost. Really, impact campaigns are about taking that emotion and the beauty of the story and the power of cinema to another level.[6]

Impact campaigns are designed to use film as a strategy to galvanize change and pull chance out of the equation. Intentionally, many filmmakers and organizers join the power of visual storytelling to shift narratives with the strength of community organizing to change power dynamics. Joined at the hip, these strategically designed campaigns increase the role of film, media, and television in aiding or (sometimes) propelling social change.

It's worth stepping back in history to contrast how *The China Syndrome* and Colin Higgins's immensely popular *9 to 5* (1980), released one year later, featuring Fonda, Lily Tomlin, and Dolly Parton, generated impact. Both films were produced by Fonda's production company IPC Films but reveal a critical distinction between the approach writers and actors use to change viewpoints and the stories activists use to inspire communities to change politics. *The China Syndrome* was a popular, well-received film that elevated nuclear issues, but it was not directly connected to an organizing strategy to end the use of nuclear power, whereas *9 to 5* illustrates the power of film when it is linked to organizing.

As the Vietnam War wound down, Fonda shifted her focus to supporting women's demands for equal rights and equal pay, and she did it the way she knew best—by making a major motion picture. Building 9to5, National Association of Working Women, was always a goal for Fonda, who said years later, "The entire time that we were working on the movie I could carry in my heart that this was married to a movement."[7]

9 to 5 is a comedy about three working women who fantasize ways of dealing with a sexist and bigoted boss. The film not only helped shift public understanding of gender discrimination but also fueled new organizing by women to demand workplace equity.

During her work with the antiwar movement, Fonda befriended

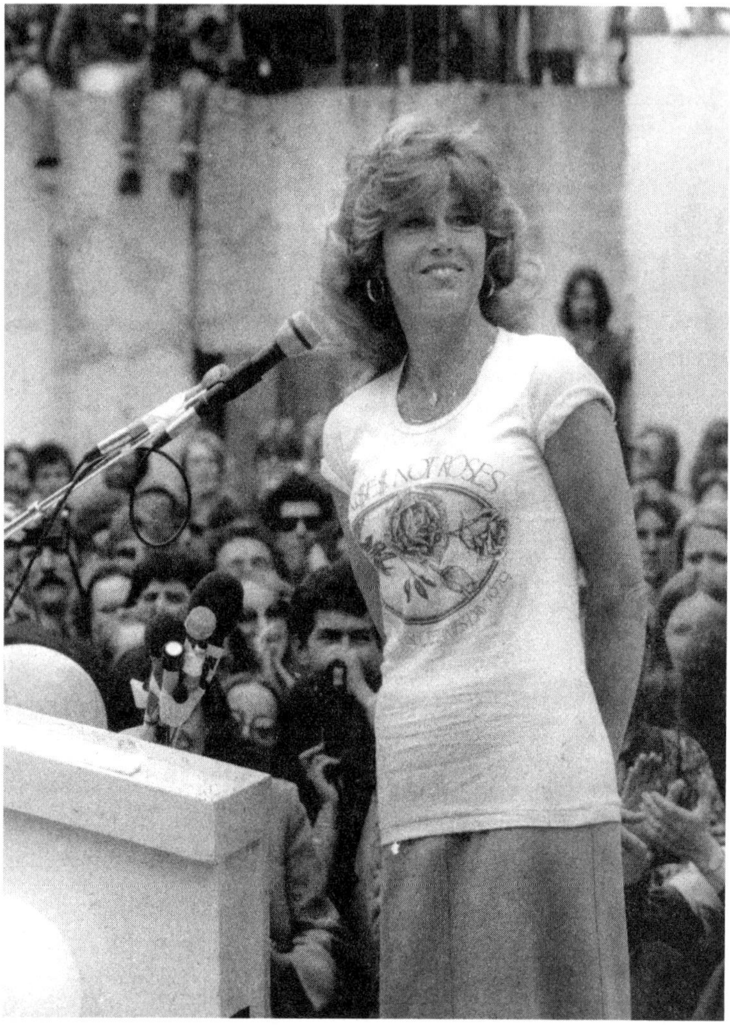

Jane Fonda encourages women workers to organize and speak out for equity at a rally held by Women Organized for Employment, the 9to5 affiliate in San Francisco, 1979. Photo by Judith Calson. Courtesy of Karen Nussbaum.

Karen Nussbaum, who co-founded 9to5, National Association of Working Woman, and invited Fonda to her organizing meetings to gain firsthand insight into the working conditions of secretaries, including their relationships with their male bosses. Fonda originally conceived of the movie as a drama. But during one pivotal meeting in Cleveland, Ohio, Fonda and Higgins asked the secretaries if anybody ever dreamed of killing their boss? Nussbaum said, "the place lit up," as each woman shared her fantasy. Some of them quite lurid: one woman wanted to grind up her boss in a coffee grinder and then serve his grounds in a hot drink. At that point, it became clear *9 to 5* needed to be a comedy, a decision they believed could enable the film to reach women who might not be drawn to a "feminist" film.[8]

9 to 5 hit home partly because the 9to5 staff advised on the development of the film script so that it reflected the real experiences of working women, rather than what Hollywood writers might imagine working women confronted.[9] The staff also provided TV screenwriters with ideas for the subsequent sitcom of the same name. This model of mutual engagement—or collaboration—among writers, actors, and community organizers has been adopted more widely by contemporary social change organizations, from the National Domestic Workers Alliance to Harness, a Los Angeles–based cultural organizing nonprofit founded by actors and producers America Ferrera, Wilmer Valderrama, and Ryan Piers Williams.

To coincide with the film's release, 9to5 organized a twenty-city tour called the Movement Behind the Movie. Thousands of women turned out for demonstrations to demand equal rights. Hundreds of women attended organizing meetings. Dolly Parton's song "9 to 5" became something of an anthem for working women, as the lyrics move from workplace pride to workplace grievance to demands for change. Its popular acclaim drove its ratings to number one on three different billboard charts and earned an Oscar nomination.[10]

Fonda did a fifteen-second Public Service Announcement for the organization connecting the fictional film landscape to long-standing inequalities and challenges faced by women in the workforce, saying, "In the *9 to 5* movie, we had a lot of fun, but you need to know how to really change the problems in your workplace. So, call this number and get your free *9 to 5* guide to office survival." Thousands of women ordered them, creating an opportunity for 9to5 organizers to follow up. Nussbaum said the "branding just exploded," and with tremendous interest in the film and the strong connection—in name affiliation and authenticity—to the organization, 9to5 quickly doubled its number of chapters.[11]

The film hit its stride in 1980 and was integral to the rapid growth of the 9to5 organization and its sister union, SEIU 925.[12] But the growth was short-lived, owing to a consequential 1980 election that brought Ronald Reagan to the presidency and an ascendant right wing into power.[13] The film jolted the women's movement, but politics, as it often does, points up the need for organizations to defend their gains by advancing their electoral interests.

Through the years, there have been a number of intentional creative collaborations that offer a blueprint for films with impact. They include community and labor organizations that embed cultural organizing in their day-to-day work or use film as an organizing tool as well as filmmakers who organize their own impact campaigns or contract with organizers to do this for them.

The fifty-year-old Chicago-based Kartemquin Films and the work of human rights filmmakers Pamela Yates and Paco de Onís reflect two of the pioneering initiatives that helped spur the many robust impact campaigns today.

Kartemquin: A Movement Building Production Company

In the mid-1960s, Kartemquin (the name derives from the merging of the last names of the three founders, Stan Karter, Jerry Temaner, and Gordon Quinn) set out to make films to critique society by analyzing power dynamics: who has power and who doesn't and how those who have power wield it in contested battles. This novel approach to filmmaking contextualized politics on a big screen in a way that lent itself to social action.

In the 1970s, they shifted their focus from making films that featured societal critiques to producing films that directly supported a wide range of campaigns and movements for change. Kartemquin evolved into a collective of organizers. Half of the collective participants came from backgrounds like teaching and union and community organizing, and some came from the media and the filmmaking community.[14] Kartemquin is among the first modern-day production companies to use film to support organizing. Their work is described by scholar-activist Patricia Aufderheide as "impact filmmaking before its time."[15]

During this period, Kartemquin supported issue campaigns and social movements by working hand in glove with community and labor organizations to design their films for impact. Early decisions in the filmmaking process were often informed by substantial discussion with organizers and community-based activists. Films were screened by community allies, who offered feedback and suggested changes.

In one film, *What's Happening at Local 70?* (1975), filmmaker Judy Hoffman documents a wildcat strike by unemployment office workers from the American Federation of State, County and Municipal Employees (AFSCME). The workers asked Kartemquin to create a film about their struggle so workers elsewhere through the city could learn what they were up against. Hoffman then told their story in their own voices, describing staff cuts and overtime pay issues during the recession of 1975. For nine weeks, Kartemquin screened and discussed the film at bars and restaurants where unemployment compensation workers congregated. Ultimately, Hoffman's film led to direct impact: the screenings led additional workers to join the union and precipitated a union-wide vote of solidarity with the striking workers that sparked a one-day strike and rally, which led to workers being rehired.

This creative process, anchored in the spirit of movement building—weaving calls to action into their films and bringing real day-to-day organizing to life to challenge systemic inequities—set Kartemquin apart from other filmmakers. Rather than trying to be "objective," these filmmakers immersed themselves in the lives of their subjects and through that immersion re-created the players and their political challenges.

In discussing the role of film collectives as a training ground for progressive filmmakers, Sonya Childress and Natalie Bullock Brown noted that Kartemquin, among others, laid "the ideological foundation and pipeline for leadership within today's documentary film spaces."[16]

Filmmakers Driving Impact

Shortly after Kartemquin got up and running, an increasing number of activist filmmakers began organizing their own impact campaigns. Such was the case with Pamela Yates's award-winning film *When the Mountains Tremble* (1983) about the genocide in Guatemala in the early 1980s. The film served as one of many "coalescing tools for non-Indigenous Guatemalans in urban areas and the Indigenous in the highlands to build a movement" against Guatemalan dictator José Efraín Ríos Montt and his government.[17]

Clandestinely at first, Mayans, Mestizos, and Ladinos throughout Guatemala used the film to convene organizing meetings and give voice to their historical memories of what really happened in the years of the dictatorship. Viewed worldwide, the film animated an international campaign against Ríos Montt, and more than twenty years later, led human rights lawyers to ask Yates to review the film outtakes, including an interview between Yates and Ríos Montt. In his own words during the interview, Ríos Montt acknowledged he controlled the army leading the repression and that he had full knowledge of what the army was doing. Yates notes that "command responsibility" is difficult to prove, but it is an essential element to obtaining a genocide conviction. Thus, the filmed interview provided the court with key forensic evidence, inculpatory clips in 16 mm film, that lawyers used to establish Ríos Montt's guilt.[18]

Ríos Montt was sentenced to eighty years in prison for genocide and crimes against humanity. Yates said that it was a climactic moment in the courtroom, even for Ríos Montt: "When a reporter

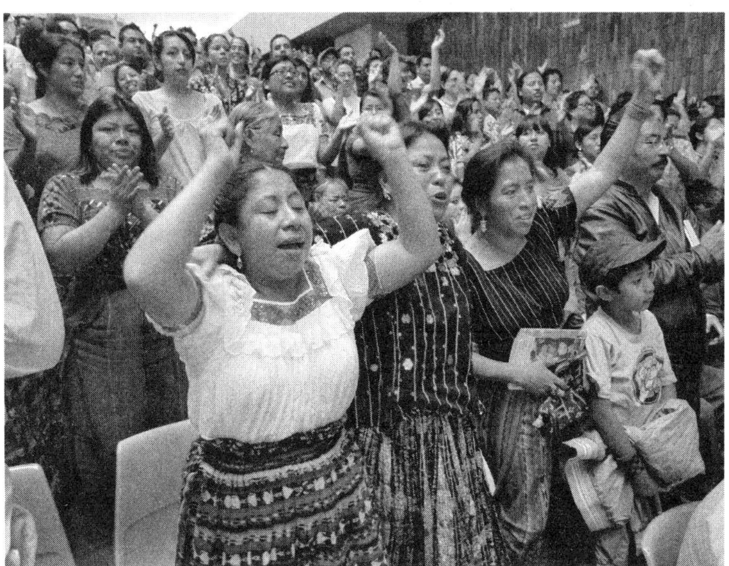

Mayan survivors of the Guatemalan genocide cheering at the guilty verdict of dictator General Ríos Montt in 2013. Photo © Daniel Hernández-Salazar from the film: "500 Years."

asked him if he remembered me or remembered doing the interview he said, 'I don't remember her, but now I'll never forget her.'"[19]

In 2005, more than two decades after the making of *When the Mountains Tremble*, a vast archive, formally known as the Historical Archive of the National Police (Archivo Histórico de la Policía Nacional), detailing the role of the police in the Guatemalan civil war was accidentally discovered. Thousands of previously secret files containing inculpatory evidence—names, addresses, and identity documents of people whom the police "disappeared"—were brought to light.[20] These evidentiary files were featured in a subsequent Yates film, called *Granito: How to Nail a Dictator* (2011), which not only joined the ascendant Mayan initiatives for justice but also prompted Black and Indigenous communities from Colombia to invite the filmmakers to their villages to help tell their stories.

Yates and the film's producer, Paco de Onís, were instrumental in bringing together Colombian filmmakers and community and movement leaders who had not previously worked with one another. In 2016, they developed SolidariLabs, weeklong intensive workshops to train activists, artists, and organizers to link film with media and movement work.[21] The labs offer organizers and filmmakers a space to exchange ideas for content and messaging and to explore real-life power dynamics that frame their work.

One distinguishing feature of the labs is their pedagogy around "relational organizing" approaches to building community, wherein activist teams of artists and community leaders develop bonds of trust and a common understanding of what working together entails.[22] This is essential, as artists and movement leaders approach the world from different perspectives. In organizer parlance, the labs reinforce the value of "building for the long term" by facilitating deeper relationships for collaboration in current and future initiatives.

The Growing Field of Impact Producers

An organization called Doc Society popularized the term "impact producer" to describe and codify the role of organizers who work with filmmakers and community and labor organizations to promote change. Founded in 2004 by Jess Search and based in London and New York, Doc Society raises money for filmmakers and their social impact teams to engage organizations and influencers allied with a film's direction and message. Previously, Search worked as a commissioning editor in the documentary department of Channel 4, in the United Kingdom, whose business-driven objectives and goals were very different from those of impact-driven filmmakers.

Community partnerships and engagement strategies were largely absent at Channel 4, and Search, a consummate professional, was frustrated that the stories she worked on had no life beyond the immediate news cycle. They would air and capture some press, and then Channel 4 would move on. In those circumstances she observes that "you wind up with a vast amount of unrealized potential left on the table."[23]

Doc Society "formally" classified an occupation and conceptualized a scope of work. They helped define "a new professional class," saying that "the Impact Producer's role varies based on the film content and defined distribution goals, but often includes overseeing a combination of strategy development, issue mapping . . . evaluation and impact measurement. . . . They are responsible for maximizing a film's potential for social change."[24]

In 2007, Doc Society introduced its pathbreaking Good Pitch event, now operating in more than thirty countries, which curates documentary film teams and introduces them to potential financial supporters. At each Good Pitch event, Doc Society presents a selection of films to an audience of national and local institutional and individual donors and an assortment of organizations working on the issues profiled in the films. With a presentation and film trailer in hand, each filmmaking team pitches for funds to their audience and to a curated stakeholders' table, which includes community organizations, analysts, artists, and donors with a vested interest in the film's message. Before the audience, "table" members discuss how the film might advance their work. In short, Good Pitch facilitates potential collaborations with hundreds of organizations that embrace new film initiatives and since its inception has raised $33 million for the film teams.[25]

Discussing film as a complement to organizing, Doc Society writes,

> [Most] filmmakers don't write policy recommendations, we introduce new narratives, voices and information so that policy recommendations can be understood in a new light. We create cultural moments, or we tie storytelling to such moments, to open opportunities for people to make new connections. And that collective energy opens the space for change to happen—a snowball effect for more stories to be told and heard, and for people who have the will to seize the moment.[26]

How It Happens

Artist-activist Kristina Mevs-Apgar started her career as a young model and actress who appeared on TV shows, including *CSI: Miami* and *Law and Order*, usually playing a girl from the wrong side of the tracks. Then, drawn to politics by Barack Obama's presidential campaign and into the world of nonprofits, Mevs-Apgar signed up with the National Domestic Workers Alliance (NDWA)—the nation's largest organization of domestic workers—to elevate the cultural strategies that NDWA has deployed almost since its inception. Mevs-Apgar said simply, "My dual lives informed each other."

Organizations like Doc Society lean in from the creative and artistic production perspective, and a growing number of social justice nonprofits are integrating cultural organizing and creative narrative strategies into their traditional organizing work. But many still consider it a "soft" strategy for reform, by which they typically mean it's "possible" culture shift work will yield progress, but they are not convinced there is sufficient evidence to conclude it is effective. These organizations may be risk averse because their budgets are not ample. Many social change organizations that embrace cultural organizing layer this work on top of other organizing, so it's inherent potential may go unrealized; however, others center narrative and organizing strategies in the mix of their campaign planning to achieve success.

Founded in 2007 by Ai-jen Poo, NDWA is an organizing center representing a portion of the more than two million domestic workers in the United States. These are largely women of color and immigrants who organize for a living wage and workplace protections, such as paid time off and overtime pay.[27] Domestic workers, including nannies, house cleaners, and home-care workers, enter the fight for political and economic rights using nontraditional labor organizing tactics, given that their workplace is often a private residence. Because each employee has a different employer and works in a separate location, taking collective political action means overcoming higher hurdles than those in other types of organizing might face.

These workers are seen only by the families who hire them, so their lack of public visibility is one of their highest hurdles and makes their capacity to organize public support more difficult. This was a particularly salient issue during the coronavirus pandemic, when in

2020 the Centers for Disease Control (CDC) and state governments established criteria to determine eligibility for priority COVID-19 vaccinations.[28]

NDWA's long-term strategy for success hinges partially on its ability to bring domestic workers out of the shadows and to reshape public opinion about them and their work. Who are domestic workers? What are the dominant narratives that define them? Are their work demands just? NDWA's challenge is to respond to these questions in a way that reframes the dominant class, race, and gender stereotypes domestic workers face. This is where film and cultural organizing enter the picture.

Ai-jen Poo argues that "having cultural strategies embedded in a social movement means you can exponentially increase your impact in the real world, because you can leverage culture change strategies with others, and connect mass audiences to policy and technology solutions that are in motion already."[29]

Art is part of everyday life. It is, as Norman Lear said, "clearly a part of everybody's expression."[30] This was evident in the collaboration between NDWA and writer-director Alfonso Cuarón, whose 2018 Academy Award–winning film *Roma* tells the story of Cleo, an Indigenous domestic worker in Mexico City who cleans the home and unconditionally cares for her wealthy employers' four children. Set in the 1970s and shot in black and white, with grit and beauty, the protagonists, played by Yalitza Aparicio (Cleo) and Nancy Garcia (Adela, the family cook), are caught up in their employers' marital difficulties while navigating their own personal relationships, including Cleo's unexpected pregnancy and abandonment by the unborn baby's callous father. Cleo is shown doing laundry, cleaning up dog feces, and caring for the children from dawn to dusk. On an outing to the beach toward the end of the film, Cleo rescues one of the children from drowning.

By simply and sympathetically depicting their quiet and heroic lives, Cuarón's story shatters stereotypes of these workers and what they do. His film presented NDWA with a strategic opportunity to affirm their members' dignity and the essential value of their work, and it opened new organizing opportunities.

The backstory of NDWA's collaboration with Cuarón exemplifies the important brokering role of media funders. Participant Media, a Jeffrey Skoll enterprise dedicated to using pop culture to foster activism and alter how we approach social issues, facilitated their relationship by inviting NDWA to attend the *Roma* premiere at the Venice Film Festival. Founded in 2004, Participant helped launch a number of impact-oriented and Academy Award–winning films, such as *An Inconvenient Truth*, which former vice president Al Gore wrote to spark action on alternatives to fossil fuels.

Participant cultivated the crucial linkage between NDWA and Cuarón that enabled NDWA to use the film as an organizing and education tool. With the Netflix release in November 2018 and with Participant's support, NDWA rolled out its social impact campaign.

The goals of NDWA's campaign were to "increase the visibility and value of domestic workers in popular culture and accelerate the adoption of solutions that concretely support security and dignity for domestic workers."[31]

The campaign succeeded in lifting the workers' spirits. Their sense of self and pride in seeing workers like themselves on the big screen mattered. Film rarely portrays domestic workers and other women of color as protagonists, and when they are seen, they're usually cast in stereotype by white male directors. In his acceptance speech at the Oscars, Cuarón thanked the academy

> for recognizing a film centered around an indigenous woman, one of the 70 million domestic workers in the

> world without work rights. As artists, our job is to look where others don't.[32]

NDWA seized on the semiautobiographical story of Cuarón's life to raise the profile of domestic workers. Millions of people watched the film and another 25 million saw Cuarón talk at the Academy Awards about the dignity of domestic work. First and foremost, NDWA's awards strategy gave these workers presence; they could be seen worldwide. Mevs-Apgar notes,

> We hosted an Oscar party in LA with hundreds of domestic workers, influencers and over 80 percent of our press hits came from that event alone. Alongside the event, we had an ambitious press and digital push. We also had prepped Alfonso [Cuarón] with talking points, and he used them during his Best Director speech/win. It was a lot of work, a huge gamble, and a big win![33]

NDWA sponsored community screenings for some 2,200 domestic workers, which served as education forums and a base-building initiative. The notion of using film for education and organizing is old, rooted for instance in the work of the 1930s Workers Film and Photo League, which used film and photography for social change, and thirty years later in Kartemquin's approach, which explicitly created and used film to support social movements. The primary difference is that NDWA was not set up as a film organization but rather as a labor organization working on behalf of domestic workers and incorporating film into its strategy.

One-third (more than seven hundred) of the workers who attended the community screenings signed up as new NDWA members. The organization's digital presence jumped dramatically as a result of the millions reached via social media. The film helped to pierce preconceived notions of low-wage women workers of color and gave recognition to their essential role in society.

This type of collaboration, wherein cultural organizing is embedded as a fundamental component of social justice organizing, illustrates how artists and organizers authentically share common ground that can be mutually rewarding. Cuarón offered a lesson to artists who want to partner with community organizations:

> To do this in a genuine way, all you do is put yourself at the service of the [social impact] organization you're working with. . . .Not trying to tell them what to do, but actually for them to lead. . . . It has to be a genuine commitment, coming from the standpoint of honesty.[34]

Using Power Analysis to Advance Film's Impact

Organizers believe it's necessary to engage political allies to challenge narratives and to win political concessions from those who hold power. Their strategies for change are informed by analyzing individual and organizational interest and determining how much power these disparate interests can exert. In the organizing community this assessment is called a "power analysis," a tool that filmmakers are now using to link their films with the work of community organizations to bolster their impact.

Filmmaker Jeff Orlowski used a power analysis to identify organizational support (and opposition) to inform the impact campaign based on his now classic, Emmy Award–winning documentary film *Chasing Ice* (2012).

Orlowski's film brings the viewer up close to multiyear time-lapsed images of mammoth glaciers calving, retreating, and pulling away from ice mountains in Iceland, Greenland, Alaska, and Montana, as documented by *National Geographic* photographer James Balog. In one unforgettable segment, audiences witness one of the largest calving incidents ever recorded when a mountain of ice the size of lower Manhattan splits away from the ancient Greenland Ilulissat glacier, providing incontrovertible evidence of climate change for those still in denial.

In 2014, Orlowski and his impact team organized the Chasing Ice Ohio Tour to help shape public opinion about climate change, facilitate legislative action, and shift voting behavior on an issue on which political lines have long been established. Specifically, the campaign was designed to persuade Representative Pat Tiberi, a Republican and a climate change denier, to reconsider his views. Just northeast of Columbus, Ohio, Tiberi's congressional district had historically voted Republican, though in a few elections, such as in Barack Obama's presidential campaign, the district broke for Democrats. The tour focused on persuading residents in Tiberi's district that climate change is real and poses a threat to their community and on shifting Tiberi's views and ultimately his vote.

Seventy national and state-based "collaborators" rolled out the campaign, which included distributing 5,500 free copies of the *Chasing Ice* DVD with a call to action tailored to Ohioans' concerns. An array of community organizations participated, including faith-based communities, the Boy Scouts of America, and rural and urban farming organizations, as well as some businesses. Many people in these organizations had voted for Tiberi, which meant that politically the congressman had an obligation, or at least incentive, to respond, even if he opted not to change his position.

The impact team organized ninety film screenings attended by nine thousand district residents. Most screenings included an information booth with specific action requests, such as asking attendees to write a poster board message that could be delivered to Rep. Tiberi and broadcast on social media. One read, "Please acknowledge the concerns of scientists on climate change. The next generation needs you to stand tall and act."[35]

The tour yielded impressive results.[36] Based on a survey of audience members before and after viewing *Chasing Ice*, conducted by Mark Mellman, a leading national pollster, the polling indicates that the film lifted by 15–25 percent (depending on the question) the number of people in the audience who after watching the film were now more certain that climate change (1) is real, (2) is caused by human activity, and (3) is extremely important and a cause for concern.[37]

The outcome of the survey provides just one example of how film, when it is directly linked to organizing, can foster change. Following the two-and-a-half-month Chasing Ice Ohio Tour, Tiberi issued the following statement:

> A global problem requires a global solution. An effective solution requires that all countries agree to participate together. I would like to see us address climate change in a balanced manner, on as broad a front as possible.[38]

In 2017, Tiberi joined the bipartisan Climate Solutions Caucus of the U.S. House of Representatives. This geographically focused campaign led to a change in Tiberi's public position on climate change, although not yet in his voting behavior. Nevertheless, the campaign laid the groundwork for ongoing climate change organizing.

The Multiple Uses of Film to Aid Organizing

For fourteen years, Sonya Childress directed impact campaigns for Firelight Media, a nonprofit organization that supports and develops nonfiction filmmakers of color. She helped position and use documentary films about pivotal moments in American history to mentor young activists and, in Childress's words, "to bolster contemporary social justice organizing by knitting together the films into ongoing campaigns around immigrant rights, voter registration and racial justice. . . . These projects were essentially deep dives into successful organizing efforts."[39] Childress's work using film to support young activists includes organizing in connection with Stanley Nelson's Emmy-nominated *Black Panther: Vanguard of the Revolution* (2016).

Black Panther documents the rise and the fall of the Black Panther Party (BPP) in the 1960s. Using the live voices of former BPP members, FBI informants, and others, the film reframes the narratives propagated by police and FBI COINTELPRO units that set out to destroy the Panthers and confronts the police killing, brutality, and vilification of the BPP that were at the core of the party's demise.

Today, Black Lives Matter (BLM) activists confront a similar right-wing onslaught. Childress gave BLM organizers early copies of the film and used the film as a training tool to explore alternative organizing strategies and to foreshadow the type of surveillance and vilification BLM could expect from the state. In short, she used the film to connect through lines between organizing efforts then and now.

The film was scheduled for broadcast by PBS on February 16, 2016 (during Black History Month) and for release to theaters in August of that year on the fiftieth anniversary of the founding of the BPP. Nelson hit the road, speaking at screenings in twenty-two cities. He was joined on stage by local rank-and-file Panthers, who participated in Q&As with local BLM activists and former national BPP members, like Ericka Huggins and Kathleen Cleaver.[40] For many, it was the first time they had talked publicly in their community about their time as Panthers.[41] The intergenerational conversation explored the similarities and differences between the challenges of the civil rights era and the challenges faced by current BLM activists. In this campaign, the film became a tool for political education with broader audiences and an opportunity for panelists to frame historical and contemporary struggles and draw out the lessons activists learned then and now.

To achieve these goals and to promote the film, Firelight Media collaborated with a wide range of community and national organizations, including the Advancement Project, Movement for Black Lives, the Center for Constitutional Rights, and the NAACP. Childress said, "Essentially we brought these organizations together to advise us on strategy, and most continued to promote and amplify and get interest in the film."[42]

Almost a week before the film's release, world superstar Beyoncé performed in the halftime show of Super Bowl 50, paying homage to the Black Panthers by celebrating their fiftieth anniversary just fifty miles from Oakland, California, where the party was founded.

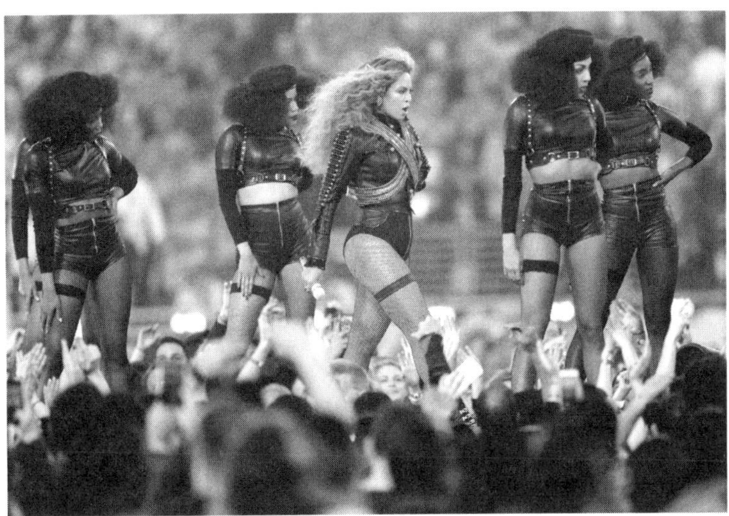

In black leather outfit and a bandolier around her torso, her dancers in black leather and berets, Beyoncé performed at the halftime show of the 2016 Super Bowl, around the time of the fiftieth anniversary of the founding of the Black Panther Party. (Photo by Ben Liebenberg/AP.)

Beyoncé and her dance crew, dressed in black leather outfits and the well-known Panther black beret, raised the Black Power fist salute in unison. Dancers formed an X on the football field, and Beyoncé wore a bandolier across her torso in an X, invoking the history of Malcolm X and the BPP.

Los Angeles Times staff writer Randall Roberts characterizes the song Beyoncé performed, "Formation," as being about "her looks, her ancestry and her identity."[43] Jenna Wortham, a *New York Times Magazine* writer, said, "'Formation' isn't just about police brutality—it's about the entirety of the black experience in America in 2016, which includes standards of beauty, (dis)empowerment, culture, and the shared parts of our history."[44]

Beyoncé's Super Bowl performance cast fresh light on police brutality and elevated the discussion of the ongoing fight for racial justice. In the wake of her performance, the *Black Panther: Vanguard of the Revolution* film release rocketed through social media. Its hashtag (#BlackPantherPBS) trended globally on Twitter, it broke viewership records for *Independent Lens*, and it brought an unprecedented number of Black viewers to PBS.[45]

The performance and film also sparked a backlash. Unhappy NFL fans organized a boycott against Beyoncé, and the police unions, which accused Beyoncé of supporting "cop killers," advised their members not to provide security for her at subsequent performances. Childress notes that "the police union's 'cop killing' narrative was now back in the news."[46]

Firelight Media ramped up its campaign by engaging activist filmmaker and writer dream hampton, who solicited high-profile Black artists to contextualize Beyoncé's performance and address questions about the legacy of the Black Panther Party. Their goal in the week between the Super Bowl and the national PBS broadcast of the movie was to reframe the narrative around the BPP as a militant fringe group, to show that the conditions that led to the Panthers were the same that were driving young people into the Movement for Black Lives, which was a nascent coalition at the time.[47] Leading up to the broadcast, they organized a teach-a-thon on Twitter to dispel myths about the Panthers that made it easier for Panthers and their active supporters, including Chaka Khan, Nile Rodgers, Mia Farrow, Kerry Washington, John Legend, Questlove, political operative Donna Brazile, Black Lives Matter co-founder Alicia Garza, and former Panthers to use their high-profile platforms to counter the cop-killer narrative and to put racial justice squarely into context.

Though it was not coordinated with the opening of *Black Panther*, Nelson later said, "There's no way I can separate myself as a filmmaker from Beyoncé's performance."[48] The concurrence of events sparked audience curiosity and fueled activists' ability to reshape public ideas about the Panthers, civil rights, and the Movement for Black Lives. It lifted up the visibility of the film to BLM activists, who used it and subsequent meetings between them and the Panthers to inform their movement strategies. Cultural activism became a force in the battle of ideas.

A long-standing and increasingly popular field of practice, tactical alliances between makers and organizers can influence public and private sector practice and policy. These collaborations, bolstered (and sometimes thwarted) by new technologies and accessibilities (e.g., streamers and social media), enable organizers and makers to reach new audiences on a large scale and to penetrate the body politic more deeply. As makers and organizers jointly consider their respective strategies for change, they can tap into the potential for high-quality documentaries and fictional films to make a difference.

4

"No Papers, No Fear"

Cultural Strategies for Migrant, Immigrant, and Refugee Justice

We don't think it's possible for our organizing campaigns to succeed without arts and culture.

—Pablo Alvarado[1]

In 2010, Arizona was the epicenter of anti-immigrant campaigns. Its state legislature passed SB 1070 (dubbed the "show me your papers" law), which required state law enforcement officials to determine the immigration status of anyone they suspected of being in Arizona without legal authorization. Widely considered the strictest anti-immigrant law in the nation, the intent of SB 1070 was to "identify, prosecute and deport" undocumented immigrants.[2]

The legislation gave law enforcement representatives, like Maricopa County sheriff Joe Arpaio, new and frequently used power to abuse and detain anybody with black or brown skin. The ACLU explained,

> Arpaio was recently convicted of criminal contempt after he deliberately violated an earlier court ruling that ordered his department to end its practice of illegally

"No Papers, No Fear" is an activist expression of undocumented immigrants that is also used as a slogan for the Undocubus, a bus filled with undocumented immigrants who traveled to the 2012 Democratic National Convention to press Democrats to stop deportations and create a pathway to citizenship.

> detaining people based only on suspicions about their immigration status. That ruling came in a successful case brought by Latino residents to challenge Arpaio's racial profiling policies.[3]

Arizona's SB 1070, which prompted other red-state legislatures and governors to introduce and pass copycat laws, reignited a national immigration reform movement. Proclaiming "No Papers, No Fear," undocumented activists stepped up their organizing for a path to citizenship. Risking deportation, three undocumented immigrants sat in Arizona senator John McCain's office in 2010, calling on him to open a path to legal status for young undocumented immigrants, the first of many Dreamers who put it all on the line.[4]

Artists, journalists, and organizers launched a fierce counter-campaign to SB 1070. Their stories offer a glimpse into the growing number of mobilization strategies that blend culture and politics, shape immigrant narratives, and draw from the earlier movement-building approaches of the Student Nonviolent Coordinating Committee (SNCC), the United Farm Workers (UFW), and others.

Organizing for Power

One of the organizations on the front lines was the National Day Laborer Organizing Network (NDLON), whose unique approach to organizing places art and culture at the heart of their strategies.

Founded in 2001 by Pablo Alvarado, a former day laborer and a musician who started the Los Jornaleros del Norte (the Day Laborer Band), NDLON organizes to improve the lives of day laborers, migrants, and low-wage workers and builds leadership among their members to confront injustices. Through fifty community affiliates and day laborer centers across the United States, they assist workers seeking employment, litigate on their behalf, fight for basic labor protections, and offer popular education programs, emphasizing nonviolent confrontation and peaceful resistance.

NDLON's thirty-five-person staff (which includes poets, musicians, a cartoonist, and an illustrator) use art to give them a tactical organizing advantage. Cartoonists, for example, make content easier to understand, particularly for workers who do not know how to read or who have limited education. The cartoons help teach people their rights, such as those they have when standing on a sidewalk waiting to be selected for day work and when interacting with police officers. One cartoon, by C. Perez, features an authoritative-looking arm and hand pointing at a day laborer and saying "Show me your papers, brown skin." The worker replies, "Here's my papers, the Constitution."[5]

In addition to hiring staff artists, NDLON works with other artists involved in immigrant justice work, including award-winning filmmaker Alex Rivera, who, among other videos, made "Wake Me Up" in 2013 with singer-songwriter Aloe Blacc, which reached number one on the charts in sixty-three countries. On YouTube, the video has been viewed more than 29 million times.[6]

NDLON and its Arizona member, Tonatierra, worked with Ernesto Yerena Montejano to create Alto Arizona, an online initiative that asked artists to denounce SB 1070. Responses came rapidly, generating five hundred posters, including Poonam Whabi's *Ain't No Border High Enough*, which featured monarch butterflies soaring above and across barbed wire, and Julio Salgado's *No Papers, No Fear*, which activists used to push Democrats to end deportations.

Just as the Committee on Chicano Rights used visual artist Yolanda López's iconic poster *Who's the Illegal Alien, Pilgrim?* (1978) to galvanize opposition to then president Jimmy Carter's immigration plan, NDLON asked artist-activists Ernesto Yerena Montejano and

Shepard Fairey to create the *Not One More* poster. This poster was reminiscent of NDLON's #Not1More Deportation campaign, which referred to the effort to end immigrant deportations and 287(g), a section of the U.S. Immigration and Nationality Act that deputizes state and local police officers to stand in as a proxy for federal ICE agents.

NDLON's visual campaign built on a deep history of using public art installations to help galvanize protest. The twentieth-century Mexican muralists David Siqueiros, Diego Rivera, and José Orozco poured their energy into the production of political posters and prints, which were widely reproduced and distributed in support of the Mexican Revolution. Those artists helped shape postrevolutionary society in Mexico by creating large murals championing the revolution and the principles underlying it. The bold, muscular figures depicted in the art evoke the resilience of the Indigenous culture, while the fact that anonymous laborers are represented at the same scale as recognizable leaders like Emiliano Zapata boosts the pride of the ordinary viewer. The Aztec-influenced style glorifies the beauty of working-class culture and served as a communication vehicle to reach a wider number of Mexicans, many of whom were poor and partly or wholly illiterate and could not be reached through the media and written materials.

Hundreds of musicians also responded to NDLON'S call, including Los Jornaleros del Norte, who produced two albums for the campaign: *Hazte Contar* and *Que No Pare la Lucha*. Reflecting the sheer grit of NDLON and their grassroots approach to organizing, accordion and keyboard player Omar Leon said,

> Norte's songs have been born in the streets, on corners and in marches, just by listening to what people say and chant, and by spending time with mothers, fathers, and youth who've suffered because of deportations, wage

> theft, even physical attacks for wanting to organize themselves.[7]

Music was a core part of NDLON's organizational culture, a way for workers to connect and bond at meetings and events. Musicians figured prominently in the 2010 summer demonstrations against SB 1070. Rage Against the Machine's front man Zack de la Rocha led a musicians' boycott of Arizona called Sound Strike. Colombian folk rock singer Juanes, musical producer and award-winning musician DJ Spooky, and comedian Chris Rock boycotted the state, while Los Lobos, Hall & Oates, and others canceled their shows. Martin Cizmar, a music critic with the Phoenix alternative weekly *New Times*, pulled together seventeen Arizona artists to produce an album of protest songs against SB 1070 entitled *A Line in the Sand*, whose proceeds went to organizations fighting the law.[8]

In 2012, NDLON and allied organizations like Tonatierra got on a bus they called the Undocubus, which bore the slogan "Sin Papeles, Sin Miedo; Jornada por la Justicia" (No Papers, No Fear; Journey for Justice). Undocumented immigrants filled the bus in Arizona and made stops in ten cities in the southern United States, between Phoenix and Charlotte, North Carolina, to speak out against U.S. immigration policies. The bus tour ended at the Democratic National Convention.[9]

At stops along the way, visual artists like César Maxit conducted more than a dozen training programs for NDLON on how to cut stencils and create posters to extend their communications reach. In the absence of a local organizing center, he recalls conducting one of the communications trainings on the top of washing machines at a Georgia laundromat where organizers were meeting. Photos from the press coverage featured monarch butterflies painted on the side of the bus. This motif, a universal symbol of migration and freedom, became identified as a global sign of resistance and hope.

Taken together, the posters, cartoons, music, and visual art forms used by NDLON and others help build and sustain the cultural identity of day laborers and their families while highlighting their heritages. Connecting immigrants through popular culture was and remains a core part of NDLON's organizing strategy. Alvarado offers this background:

> What happens is when you're a worker and your wages are stolen, you're mistreated. When you're an immigrant and you don't have papers, just that fact of not having documents puts you in a vulnerable position, not just in front of society, but within yourself. You don't feel that you fit, you feel that you are a burden, you feel that you are an outsider all the time. So in order to organize and to make sure that people defend themselves when they are subjected to oppression, to difficult situations, you have to elevate the self-esteem.
>
> You have to build a cultural identity that people feel that they belong to. Because when you have that, when you have a strong cultural root, cultural background and identity, it's very difficult for an employer to come and rob you of your wages. To us, using arts and culture is a matter of building that kind of power. You cannot build real power unless people have an incredible sense of self-regard, self-love. This is why we incorporate art.[10]

Artists Enlist Artists

In 2011, as immigrant rights organizers accelerated their campaign against SB 1070, a small team of artists and cultural strategists organized a delegation of fifty acclaimed visual, literary, and performing artists, including comedian W. Kamau Bell, visual artist Wangechi

Mutu, and filmmaker dream hampton, to travel to Arizona to learn about immigration.[11] This delegation, which became known as CultureStrike, aimed to draw artists more deeply in the ongoing immigrant rights campaign and to create new artwork to help shift the many false narratives that frame popular views of immigrants.

Favianna Rodriguez, an Oakland-based visual artist and one of CultureStrike's founders, described part of their immersive experience:

> We took artists to see the Pima County Medical Examiner's Office. At that time, there were a lot of freezers because there were so many border crossings and people dying [from their journey across the desert]. We took them to see Operation Streamline, which is where [in one 90-minute session] seventy migrants would get deported at one time. They all had chains at their feet. We took them to meet with groups like the Florence Immigrant and Refugee Rights Project.[12]

The trip gave artists the opportunity to learn from one another. It connected prominent artists, such as celebrated authors Maxine Hong Kingston and Jessica Hagedorn, with a younger generation of emerging artists and Dreamers, creating valuable connections among them.

The Arizona trip had a lasting impact on Rodriguez, who a year later created the now ubiquitous *Migration Is Beautiful* poster, featuring a monarch butterfly whose wings contain human profiles. Thumbing through her archives, one can see more than a half dozen variations in form, color, and background of this image, which directly challenges the popular images of the U.S. immigration system and symbolizes freedom. *See Plate 2.* Rodriguez's website describes it this way:

> Like the monarch butterfly, human beings cross borders to survive. The phrase, "Migration is Beautiful," celebrates the resiliency, courage, and determination of migrants who come in search of their dreams.[13]

The monarch butterfly image is used frequently by artists and immigrant rights advocates. DC-based artist-activist César Maxit created a version entitled *Migrant: All Humans Have a Right to Migrate, All Migrants Have Human Rights* in which he drew a fist into each quadrant of the butterfly wings. Some activists printed, wheat-pasted, and stenciled the butterfly on to public fixtures to lift its message. Others created monarch butterfly puppets and chalk murals.

Teachers from the National Education Association (NEA) began requesting guides for creating posters and butterfly wings for use in classrooms. Ten years later, the symbol's use in schools continues to spread, including at Linder Elementary School, in Austin, Texas, which gave local artists a green light to paint monarch butterflies on its exterior walls to "honor migration and immigrant communities."[14]

Visual arts have become part of the fabric of immigrant rights organizing. Works by artists like Paola Mendoza illustrate how art also helps shape immigrant narratives. In 2021, artist-activist and award-winning filmmaker and author Mendoza conceived of and created work to advance the Immigrants Are Essential campaign launched by the National Immigration Law Center (NILC) and Resilience Force. They commissioned a variety of art, including billboards and posters, in ten different cities to amplify the essential role of immigrants, with the aim of adding new voices to demand a pathway to citizenship for eleven million undocumented workers.[15] Mendoza states,

> They've taken care of our children; they've worked in the hospitals, whether that be as nurses and doctors or as cleaning staff. They've worked in transportation to transport the food that got to our table. They're farmers picking the blueberries to put on our table—and many of them have died.[16]

First, Mendoza interviewed the families of seven undocumented immigrants who died during the COVID-19 pandemic while doing their jobs. Gutted by the human toll of the pandemic and seeing rows of empty storefronts as "the first manifestation of our loss," Mendoza printed beautiful portraits of the workers she learned about and pasted their images on a large storefront window in the Soho neighborhood of New York City. In Washington, DC, the portraits covered the windows of Roost, a culinary clubhouse on Capitol Hill. In Phoenix, they were displayed at the Latino Arts and Cultural Center, and in Los Angeles at Community Made. Using QR (quick response) codes, a passerby could listen to the stories of these workers as told by their friends and family members. Immigrants Are Essential exemplifies how visual artists can simultaneously honor the lives of those in the immigrant community and tackle the narratives that minimize them.

Digital Art Propels Activism

By 2016, the surge of art connected to immigrant organizing was accelerated by the Trump administration's now infamous racist attacks on Mexicans ("rapist and thugs"), on Africans ("shithole countries"), on Muslims ("terrorists"), and on virtually anybody who was not white. Fighting over the border wall boosted the platform of Trump's shady QAnon followers—conspiracy theorists who believe "the world is run by a cabal of Satan-worshipping pedophiles"—and the likes of Representative Paul Gosar (R-AZ), who animated his desire via social media to kill Congresswoman Alexandria Ocasio-Cortez.[17] Threatened by racial justice organizing, Trump gave voice to those on the right who demonize immigrants, in the hope that racist appeals to his white base would lead to partisan gain. In order to fight back, artists wielded art, in the words of poet and playwright Bertolt Brecht, "not as a mirror held up to reality, but a hammer with which to shape it."[18]

Social media and new technologies gave rise to new forms of collaboration among immigrant rights organizations and artists. Organizations like United We Dream, whose online database reaches nearly four million people, offer migrant artists a vehicle to infuse their work into social movements.

Ernesto Yerena Montejano, in collaboration with Amplifier, an organization that embraces art to amplify social movements, created an augmented reality (AR) poster called *Redefine*, a portrait of immigrant rights organizer and attorney Lizbeth Mateo Jimenez. In capital letters Yerena Montejano wrote "REDEFINE" across the top of the poster and Amplifier then layered her voice over her image. Pointing a mobile phone app at the image of Jimenez allows the viewer to hear her saying, "Under no condition, especially one of a broken system, will we accept the denial of a full life. We are architects of community, builders of legacy. We refuse to live a small life."[19]

Along with a lesson plan, the *Redefine* poster was sent to twenty thousand educators and used by more than a million students as a source for discussion about immigration.[20] Explaining AR, scholar

Ronald Azuma noted that it "allows the user to see the real world with virtual objects superimposed or composited with the real world. . . . It supplements reality rather than comprehensively replacing it, as with Virtual Reality."[21]

Julio Salgado, among the most notable of the undocumented digital artists, said he "came of age with social media. It started with Myspace, then Facebook and now with Instagram . . . it's an easier way just to put work out there."[22] For undocumented artists, it also creates an opportunity to circulate their art without risking arrest in jurisdictions that make it illegal to wheat-paste posters and signs or paint murals on public and private property. It's a safer space for them to work in, and it boosts the potential impact of their contributions.

Both undocumented and queer, Salgado is a prolific blogger, political cartoonist, and graphic illustrator. Hard copies of his digital art are frequently printed to create murals and posters for social action and are installed in such places as the Mission District of San Francisco, home to many immigrants who live in the city. Perhaps his most well-known work, created in collaboration with Galería de la Raza, is called *I am UndocuQueer*, portraits of six LGBTQ undocumented activists who penned self-affirming statements on their T-shirts, including "UndocuQueer is more than a Hashtag. It's my Identity" and "There is no thing as a single-issue struggle because we don't live single-issue lives" (quoting poet Audre Lorde).

Salgado makes art that other people can see themselves in.[23] Recognition of gay and undocumented communities and self-affirmation of one's identity are recurrent themes in his work. He shifts the narrative of his communities from one of victimhood to one of a social force, reprising the issues elevated by NDLON and other immigrant rights organizations with which he collaborates.

In a 2019 collaboration with the Inland Coalition for Immigrant

Justice, in Ontario, California, located in the Inland Empire region of Southern California, Salgado helped create and organize the Flowers on the Inside letter and postcard campaign to challenge immigrant detention practices.

The coalition is trying to close the Adelanto Detention Facility, the largest ICE detention center in the United States, where 2,700 immigrants are locked up. They accuse the city of Adelanto of expanding its detention facility to secure lucrative ICE contracts.

Salgado's Flowers on the Inside project linked undocumented immigrants held inside Adelanto to their communities. Salgado and four other undocumented artists designed postcards, which several thousand people sent to individuals detained inside the facility to express solidarity.

In the beginning, Salgado was not sure what an image could really do or even if it could make a difference. He solicited advice from undocumented artists who had been detained previously, and they said,

> When you are in a detention center, you feel like you're just a number, like you are almost nobody. Getting letters from people outside is a life changer for folks inside.[24]

The postcard and letter-writing campaigns expressed compassion and concern for those detained and became part of the campaign to close Adelanto, but it also reflected artist-driven work that builds solidarity, an essential ingredient to building power. In 2020, as the fight continued, a fleet of skytyping planes took to the skies over detention facilities with aerial messages, part of a national project of eighty artists who created the In Plain Sight campaign, wherein artists created numerous water vapor messages that could be seen for miles surrounding some eighty different detention facilities across the United States.[25] Over Adelanto, the message was simple: "Free Them All."

Building Power Through Literary Arts and Journalism

Inspired by young undocumented activists whose public interactions could put them at risk of arrest and deportation, Pulitzer Prize–winning journalist and film and theater producer Jose Antonio Vargas launched the narrative change organization Define American in 2011 by publishing a widely read op-ed in the *New York Times Magazine* in which he "outed" himself as an undocumented immigrant journalist for the *Washington Post*. Like the undocumented youth who inspired him, Vargas worried that publicly identifying himself in this way could paint a target on his back. Undeterred, he collected stories of how people define "American" and what it means to be undocumented in the United States. Through these firsthand stories, Vargas hopes to transform how undocumented immigrants and immigration are discussed in popular discourse.

These stories became part of an early-stage initiative that included funders and racial justice, arts, and other activist organizations working to create an alternative media infrastructure to counter the media ecosystem developed by the right wing to spin anti-immigrant narratives. Define American initially set out to influence entertainment, media, and news reporting by consulting with writers who create content for films and TV and by bringing immigrants directly into writers' rooms to talk with screenwriters about their lived experience. In this way, Define American and a wide range of social justice organizations are helping to shape how immigrants are perceived in popular culture.

In addition to placing more authentic voices in writers' rooms for fictional stories, Define American also helps reporters speak with individuals directly affected by U.S. immigration policies and practices, working to correct biased language and tropes. In 2013, the Associated Press and the *Los Angeles Times* dropped the term "illegal" when referring to undocumented immigrants—a phrase that was intentionally introduced as a politically motivated strategy to sway audiences against comprehensive immigration reform. More recently, in 2021, President Biden directed two federal agencies, the Customs and Border Protection (CBP) and ICE, to stop referring to migrants as "aliens." These changes followed pressure campaigns, such as Race Forward's Drop the I-Word campaign, which targeted journalist audiences based on research about the use of the i-word.[26] Eliminating prejudicial language is change.

In Define American's artist fellowship program, the fellowships come with a small no-strings-attached stipend that creates space for artists to freely express themselves unencumbered by fixed demands. In the end, it is an investment without parameters in the promise of an artist's work and an affirmation of the artist themselves. Concerned that undocumented immigrants are already limited by borders, Vargas said the last thing he wanted to do is "create even more borders by being so prescriptive."[27]

For the years 2016 to 2018, Define American selected poet Yosimar Reyes to be its first artist in residence. Born in Guerrero, Mexico, Reyes grew up mostly in East San Jose, California, undocumented, queer, and tired of the "oppression narrative" that is pervasive in storytelling about gay and undocumented individuals. Reyes wrote "UndocuJoy," a poem, later produced as a video, that inspired other artists and his community to focus on their resilience, strength, and love.

UndocuJoy

I love my undocumented people.
I love us because every day we wake up to a country that hates us.
We wake up, give thanks to God, and go to work.
Watch the news, hear how our own TVs vilify us.
We change the channel and pray that tomorrow will be a better day for us.
When they give us a little breathing room, we make the most of it.
We're so grateful that often we forget we deserve better
that all this mess is not our fault.
We stay low on the radar, want peace, want to exist without the added stress of having to be public about where our spirits ache.
We just want to go to work to feed our families,
yet we become scapegoats to a system that is addicted to exploiting the poor.
I love my undocumented people
because the way our spirits are toyed with, you need some unfathomable strength.
I love us because we have constantly had to prove our humanity and constantly done it beautifully
because to stay human under these conditions, you have to have an understanding of beauty.
I love us, even when our stories are manipulated and exploited, even when we are presented gloom and doom narratives.
I love us because at the end of the day,

somehow, we always manage to make something out of nothing.
I love my undocumented people
because being undocumented is not political.
It's not physical.
It is a condition created to keep us from smiling.
But look at us thriving.[28]

Reyes said, "I wrote 'UndocuJoy' not because I wanted to say that undocumented lives are joyful but to remind undocumented people that there are moments in our lives that we should honor and treasure, and moments in which we do experience joy, in which we do forget about our [undocumented] status."[29]

The poem invokes in listeners the kind of self-love and self-regard that Pablo Alvarado discussed as a necessary precondition to succeed in organizing. Teachers now use "UndocuJoy" in their classrooms, and nonprofit advocates and undocumented resource centers include Reyes's poem in their video presentations and literature. It spurred the Kresge Foundation to fund three six-person artist cohorts at Define American.

Define American and a constellation of arts and narrative change organizations are learning how to facilitate collaboration with organizers who are not artists but who are part of community and labor organizations that have the infrastructure and resources to lead policy and legislative campaigns. Increasingly, activists are coming to recognize that linking storytelling with advocacy campaigns is an effective way to both change public perceptions and take on powerful interests. At the Center for Cultural Power, Salgado oversees a fellowship program geared toward undocumented, LGBTQ, and disabled activists who want to write for TV because they accurately view popular culture as a means to reshape public perceptions of their communities.[30]

Storytellers can reframe our views. And Vargas reminds us that they enable us to imagine something beyond what's in front us. Indeed, he defines winning as "increasing the number of storytellers—journalists, filmmakers, authors, playwrights, musicians, and other artists—who see immigrant rights as human rights, and who see that immigrants are not only people worthy of dignity but actually an integral part of this country."[31]

Narrative work is also the subject of a 2020 Race Forward initiative called the Butterfly Lab for Immigrant Narrative Strategy. Race Forward, a multifaceted racial justice organization, launched the lab to develop approaches to (1) integrate the work of cultural strategists, artists, and communications experts with other leaders from within the organizing and legal communities and (2) vet their learnings, based on research and evaluation, with the immigrant rights community with the goal of advancing pro-immigrant narratives.

Their emerging recommendations call for investing in artists and art-led narrative projects in collaboration with advocates. Artist Aisha Shillingford, one of the narrative leaders of the Butterfly Lab, put it this way:

> We need to transform strategic communications and cultural strategy so that policy and communications folk include more imagination, feeling, and emotions in policy spaces, more dreaming and storytelling from artists. And we need artists to include more action in their work, creating socially engaged narratives accountable and responsive to movements.[32]

Social Practice

Artists, such as Chicana muralist Judith Baca and French photographer and street artist JR, have created a raft of significant work on migration and social justice that the art world recognizes as "social practice" or "participatory art." These artists collaborate with community organizations or individuals and through their engagement seek to raise public consciousness and inspire others to take stock of what they value. Like organizers who embed in their communities to cultivate relationships, artists with participatory practices see the relationship between the artist and community as integral to the artwork.

Baca, who is reprising and updating her forty-five-year-old mural dubbed *The Great Wall of Los Angeles* (1978), offers one such example. Baca engaged four hundred community-based mural makers, mostly youth from low-income neighborhoods, as well as historians and ethnologists, to trace the California history of ethnic people from prehistoric times through the 1950s.

The original project was funded with public and private money originating from businesses, foundations, religious institutions, and individuals. The Los Angeles Summer Youth Employment Program offered employment to many young muralists who had just come out of juvenile detention centers. Their colorful pictorial history presents the deep character of people who participated in campaigns for social and economic justice, from the suffragists demanding the vote to striking workers demanding better pay.

Stretching more than a half mile in the "flood control channel" across the San Fernando Valley of Los Angeles, and standing 13.5 feet high and 2,754 feet long, the mural is a historical rendering of life as seen through the eyes of Indigenous, Latino, Black, and Asian communities.

Baca's project presents an alternative to conventional narratives of California's history and cultural heritage, while at the same time helps to build community ties among those who took part in creating this cultural landmark, including rival gangs. Hector Martinez, one of the young people who helped create the mural, said, "We learned life and social skills and acceptance."[33]

To this day, the wall serves to make visible and to reaffirm California's diverse community. It reaches countless numbers of people whose views it helps to shape. In 2021, the Mellon Foundation provided a $5 million grant to restore and extend the mural. Baca, alumni from her previous team, and community activists expect to update the historical timeline in advance of the 2028 Los Angeles–based Olympics.

Likc Baca, strcct artist and photographcr JR is known for site-specific, culturally reflective, large-scale art projects, and his process is at the core of the artwork itself. He uses images to tell a story that engages the public and stirs the viewer to reimagine alternatives to the status quo. Two of JR's socially engaged collaborations featured enlarged photographs of migrants, which JR installed in highly visible places. *GIANTS, Kikito* (2017), a site-specific installation along the U.S.-Mexico border, mostly enlisted individual community members directly, and *Inside Out 11M* was staged in multiple U.S. cities, working in collaboration with community organizations committed to reforming the immigration system. JR notes that the projects have different reach and different impact.

In 2017, in Tecate, Mexico, a border community about an hour southeast of San Diego, JR installed his much-heralded *GIANTS, Kikito,* a seventy-foot-high photograph of a toddler, mounted on plywood and propped up by scaffolding, who appears to be peering out over the thirty-foot border wall, seemingly reaching over it.

JR snapped the photo of Kikito looking out from his crib when he was a year old. *See Plate 4.*

Discussing the monumental image of her baby, Kikito's mother, Lizzy Higareda, thought JR was "trying to give voice to what is silent, because we live directly on the border. He is giving a face to what many distort. . . . In a place that no one takes into account, he made it stand out, the same face that lives here that no one looked at until he made them big. . . . People have the wrong image of us, like we are the worst. I think a child does not find malice [referring to the divisions created by the border wall] when he is looking to play. He's simply observing."[34]

When JR posted a picture on his Instagram account of *Kikito* with two border patrol agents looking up at the child high above them, more than a million viewers tuned in. The image became a media sensation as Trump, newly elected, increased rhetorical attacks on immigrants. Visitors arrived from around the world to see it, while newspapers and magazines ran dozens of stories. Some of these titles include "The Art of JR Lifts a Mexican Child over the Border Wall," (*New Yorker*); "Proud to Be Mexican: Meet the Baby Whose Huge Image Gazes over the Border" (*The Guardian*); "The Art of the Border: Searching for Kikito" (*Prospect Magazine*).[35]

On the day before it was deinstalled, the baby and his family joined hundreds of community members to share a meal at an event dubbed the Giant Picnic. JR built a picnic table that stretched from both sides of the border wall, with the image of a Dreamer's eyes looking up at *Kikito*. The community shared food while musicians performed—on both sides of the wall—creating connection for a moment despite the barrier between them and, simultaneously, starkly reinforcing the division.

JR's critics do not think it went far enough. Some believe the resources that went into creating *Kikito* would have been better used in support of Mexican artists and their communities. They raise questions about the impact of an artist "parachuting" into a site to make work that did not emanate from or have longevity in that community.

Though JR personally funded the installation, it's reasonable to ask what he left behind after the installation was taken down.

Kikito was erected for a month, around the time Trump threatened to end DACA (Deferred Action for Childhood Arrivals) protections for hundreds of thousands of children brought to the United States by their parents. The installation and the work surrounding it were not linked to the on-the-ground work of activists spearheading immigration reform. But JR's art—as art often does—serves different purposes. Sometimes art can raise questions or change an individual's perceptions of issues and places, and that has public value, especially when experienced by millions.

By contrast, JR intentionally worked with the immigrant rights community when he created *Inside Out 11M* (2021) to mobilize support for federal legislation that would create a pathway to citizenship. "11M" refers to the 11 million undocumented people currently in the United States.

JR set up a photo booth inside a panel van whose side he made look like a camera, to shoot and print large black-and-white poster-size portraits of migrants and their communities. The mobile photo booth stayed one week in each of sixteen cities in seven states. Children and adults were drawn to the van as they passed by it on the street and saw the large portraits of other community members. At the same time, community organizations in each city engaged their members, patrons, and the public to call for citizenship.

The photo collage created a diverse picture of America.[36] The images were displayed side by side and stacked on top of each other on homes, retail buildings, and in front of state capitols. In Philadelphia, Kimberly Alfaro Jimenez discussed her portrait:

> I was born in Costa Rica. I am an immigrant myself on the path to citizenship, so I completely understand the

> immigrant struggle—everything it takes to be recognized and find a community here in the United States. This 11M project is super beneficial . . . it brings advocacy and exposure to these families . . . and I am more than honored to be here present in this project.[37]

In Michigan, with stops in Detroit, Grand Rapids, and Lansing, JR's team partnered with local organizers from the Michigan People's Campaign and Michigan United, both of which promote immigration reform, and with nonprofit organizations like the Detroit-based Library Street Collective, a conventional gallery space. In one portrait, a woman is seen smiling, offering hope "for a brighter future," in a T-shirt that reads, "Defend DACA: Abolish ICE: Citizenship for All."[38]

Culminating three weeks later in Washington, DC, four giant portraits of immigrants, featuring Alejandro Morales, a Dreamer; Yonas Hagos, a decorated U.S. veteran; Guadalupe Martinez, a farmworker; and Patrick Collison, a technology entrepreneur, were displayed on the front lawn of the U.S. Capitol.

The sum of the different stops involved dozens of organizations, nine thousand people who had their photos taken, and countless others who participated in street actions. TV and news reports and social media amplified their voices and refreshed their call for a pathway to citizenship.

Kikito and *Inside Out 11M* contrast two forms of social practice, one that works with individuals and another that works with community organizations. The former is oriented toward altering individual public perceptions and the press; the latter builds on a history of organizing for immigrant rights. *Kikito* garnered worldwide attention, and although it was a onetime event, it lives on through its iconic image. *Inside Out 11M* strengthened the ties among community leaders, advocates, and the public, instilling a spirit of unity and struggle. That carries on.

Obstacles to Collaboration

Artists and organizers often don't have a shared language. Organizers don't do as much storytelling as artists do, and many culture shift organizations are more focused on advancing narratives that don't directly challenge the political power arrangements that dominate policy and legislative action. Compounding these differences, artists and organizers may have varying goals and timelines for achieving change. Some artists think about impact in entirely different ways than organizers do. Visual artist Hank Willis Thomas says, "As an artist, if you only based your work off its immediate impact, you would never do anything. We've learned that impact on an artist's timeline is ten, twenty, thirty, or forty years."[39] On the other hand, art also has explosive immediate impacts, as we've seen across social movements. Author-activist Jeff Chang calls art an "accelerant for protests in the streets."[40]

Nonprofit budgets are tight, so hiring an artist whose work is not prescribed, such as in the Define American fellowship program, is a risk. It's a leap of faith that requires organizations to grapple with long-standing questions that arise when social change organizations and artist-activists join forces.

Artists value their autonomy and worry that organizations will restrain their creative impulse to fit a preconceived notion of what work will generate the most impact. Visual artist and activist Shepard Fairey notes that he may not work with some (social change) organizations in the creative stage of his practice because sometimes "they get in the way of getting something out that might be more powerful by trying to check off too many boxes in one piece of art."[41]

Organizations, on the other hand, spend time and money on poll testing and message development to create the greatest impact, and they have concerns about whether the artwork will create perceptions that fit their own messaging guidelines. This dynamic makes funding for an arts position within a social change organization rare.

The Road Forward

In an article entitled "Hopeful, 'Unapologetic' Art Rebrands the Immigration Movement," journalist Cristina Costantini remarks that "in many ways, protest art has been for the immigration movement what music was for the civil rights movement of the 1960s."[42] A long but uneven tradition has artist-activists and movement leaders using art to propel their campaigns forward by joining art, culture, and politics.

Immigrant rights activists are making a strategic choice to integrate narrative shift work through the arts with day-to-day community organizing. This forward-looking approach to social change is playing an increasingly large role in the fight for citizenship for 11 million undocumented people. Beyond legal status, many are fighting for everyone seeking refuge in the United States to be welcomed with dignity and respect. They are also deepening their collaboration across issues, including racial, environmental, and economic justice.

Working at the intersection of art and politics, immigrant rights advocates, artists, and organizers alike are developing this burgeoning area of work to shift how we organize and think about building power. Among many of their contributions, their alliances may serve as a strategic model for future movements, as narrative shift work, art, and organizing are more seamlessly blended.

5

"You Can't Be Neutral on a Moving Train"

Who Do Museums Serve?

Cultural Institutions, regardless of the subject matter, have to be as much about today and tomorrow, as they are about yesterday.

—Lonnie Bunch, Secretary, Smithsonian Institution[1]

In a *New York Times* interview, Kate Fowle, director of the Museum of Modern Art PS1, said the contemporary art museum was "using art as the center for how we build community."[2] By example, she cited the museum's Homeroom Project, which fostered community collaboration in dealing with issues such as climate justice, immigrant labor, and Black transgender identity.[3] This was music to the ears of community organizers working on the same issues. As museums increasingly center community interests, they spark new forms of community collaboration by supporting activists and critical thinking on issues ranging from housing to voting rights.

What's unclear is whether museum boards and staff will find greater collaboration advantageous or whether they are more likely to become community action targets. It's also too early to know whether community activists will find it in their interest to collaborate with museums. This chapter delves into three different models of how museums and social justice advocates work—through collab-

---

Drawn from the title of Howard Zinn's book *You Can't Be Neutral on a Moving Train: A Personal History* (Boston: Beacon, 2018).

orative or confrontational practices—to frame ideas that define our worldview. It argues that these new alliances can be a powerful driver of social justice narratives and can spur social change.

Disrupting the Status Quo

In 2020, a global pandemic transformed museums into abandoned warehouses, forcing them to shutter and absorb lost revenue from ticket sales. These eerie and existential moments pushed some museum staff and boards to reimagine their mission and how to carry it out. They produced significant changes in museum operations, including pivoting from in-person exhibitions to expanded use of social media and online programming.

The movement for Black lives that got underway in the 2010s spurred activists inside and outside the museum world to challenge pervasive cultural exclusions in museum collections, exhibitions, and hiring choices. With far more intensity than in the past, they called into question how cultural institutions address such issues as racial justice, equity, repatriation, and decolonization. They voiced concerns over which collective memories these institutions highlight, what cultural narratives they present to the public, who tells them, and the extent to which their exhibitions are a true portrayal of history or an accurate reflection of their communities.

New York Times art critic Holland Cotter, in an article entitled "Money, Ethics Art: Can Museums Police Themselves?" frames the context for activism in this way:

> In the present American political climate, with nationalism and racist, ethnic and xenophobic violence at high tide, neutrality is not an option for institutions that have ethical imperatives, represented by arts, built into their DNA. We need these institutions, which include our

> art museums, to be proactive alternative environments, in which standardized power hierarchies are dissolved, a polycultural range of voices speak, the history of art is truthfully told, and truth itself is understood as an always-developing story.[4]

Both artist-activists and community organizers have skin in the game. Artists have long used museum exhibitions to advance critical ideas and to shape public perception, from Pablo Picasso's antiwar *Guernica* to Kehinde Wiley's *Rumors of War*. But the impact of their work is limited, partly because museum audiences represent a narrow sliver of the American public. Though museums are expanding their audiences through social media, we don't yet know the impact of these communication initiatives. Visibility, though important, will not be the catalyst for change that artist-activists want.

Community organizers, like artists, have a direct stake in the role museums play in advancing ideas and using narrative strategy to contest for power. Organizers inherently understand the value of story that shapes community views and understand that their work may shift public opinion.

Using art as a central driver, collaborations among community and museum leaders can exert cultural and political influence on the lives of ordinary people. Whether these collaborations are a passing moment or are suggestive of a broader trend that contributes to tackling some of the nation's most profound and persistent issues depends in part on how deeply this work penetrates our lives. These stories cast light on the possibilities.

A Museum Hires a Community Organizer

A few museums have developed an in-depth approach to community building, a central component of all community organizing.

That was a chief aim of the New York–based Queens Museum of Art (QMA) when former director Tom Finkelpearl was intent on offering the surrounding community programming they desired. In 2006, the museum broke from tradition and hired a community organizer, Naila Caicedo-Rosario, to assess the art interests of the local communities and to develop a programming plan to serve them. This introduced a paradigm shift from one of inviting audiences to view exhibitions determined by art world experts to one of facilitating partnerships between museums and the local community to determine how and what art exhibitions and programs would best serve their interests and needs.

Finkelpearl said Caicedo-Rosario brought a skill set to the museum that it didn't have previously. Her experience with ACORN and the Working Families Party on issues such as immigration, housing, and predatory lending meant she had a deep knowledge of the issues facing the community and a wide preexisting set of relationships she could tap to build deeper levels of trust between neighborhood-based organizations and the museum.

Caicedo-Rosario said the museum job interested her because "the position was another type of organizing, not necessarily in politics, but it was the same community that I already knew."[5] At the time of her hire, community partnerships were all but absent, and QMA audiences rarely came from the local neighborhood of Corona, a section of Queens, New York, with a relatively low-income Latinx immigrant community composed mostly of Colombians, Ecuadorians, Mexicans, and Dominicans, many of whom speak different types of Spanish and often did not speak with one another.[6] It was critical that Caicedo-Rosario not only spoke Spanish but also spoke the social and cultural language of Corona.

Finkelpearl and Caicedo-Rosario summarize their partnership by recounting the development of a ten-year program to restore Corona Plaza from the site of small one-off museum-sponsored events and street fairs into a renovated public space and central location for the museum's public art projects, community festivals, parks, and public space advocacy work. The plaza is now a highly visible gathering spot that draws in community organizations, elected officials, health care providers, artists, and a fair number of demonstrations.

According to the museum,

> We needed to earn the neighborhood's trust, so that Corona residents would feel that the Queens Museum wanted to be a long-term partner, that we weren't just there for self-promotion. This is the difference between outreach and community organizing. Instead of us bringing in already planned art projects, the community organizer was there to listen and learn. The Queens Museum looked for someone who already knew the local organizations and had established networks in the neighborhood. An organizer would also have experience canvassing—talking to residents in their homes and on the street, and meeting with local elected officials and organizations. It was important to have someone on staff who could speak in a language that community organizations, service providers, and elected officials could relate to. This was a different vocabulary than the one used in the museum world. It was also very important that the organizer spoke the languages that were most prevalent in the neighborhood. In Corona, that's Spanish.[7]

In 2007, the museum launched its Heart of Corona initiative, which began as a set of discussions with a broad cross section of community leaders and residents, from immigrant rights advocates and health center staff members, to local economic development corporations and diverse arts organizations. For three years, these discussions, hosted every few months, identified a clear, unambiguous, unmet need: residents wanted the city to better maintain Corona's streets and to create safe public spaces.

QMA staff grappled with whether it could help achieve these goals. Ultimately, Finkelpearl noted they embarked on a three-part strategy to (1) design a long-term participatory arts project that elevated the role of cultural organizations in the lives of community residents, (2) use their connections to philanthropy and their own arts budget to finance part of the work, and (3) tap political support from community leaders and elected officials to transform a section of Corona into a plaza that, in addition to art and culture, would offer community and health services. Metro Plus Health, for instance, which provides low-cost health insurance coverage to communities, identified Corona as a place that had high incidences of diabetes and high blood pressure. So providing access to health care became a critical community service.

The museum partnered with New York City Council member for Corona Julissa Ferreras, and the Department of Transportation (DOT) to de-map the area and transform it into a public plaza closed to traffic.[8] The museum created an open call for artist participation. Museum staff, and eventually community residents, served as jurors who selected varied public art projects for the plaza, including using vendor carts to engage community members in discussion as well as artists' cutouts, such as La Coronita, a mascot and animation (*Adventures of La Coronita*) that Mike Easterbrook created to highlight sites that were important to the community.[9]

Complementing the juried projects, mariachi bands and other music groups, traditional dancers reflecting the cultures of their communities, printmaking workshops, and visual artists energized the plaza. In addition to enriching the art and culture of the community, QMA and community leaders hoped to shift the narrative about Corona "from one of municipal neglect to a place where community members were shaping their neighborhoods."[10] This transformational work, led by a museum-based community organizer, was ultimately driven by artists, art organizations, and a wide range of community groups and political operatives.

The Queens Museum of Art is one model for the way museums are increasingly centering their work in community, by refocusing and prioritizing art spaces and exhibitions in service to the needs of their local neighborhood. They have continued to hire new organizers who work in their public programs and community engagement departments, not in curatorial or education.

The Arizona State University (ASU) Art Museum, under the leadership of Miki Garcia, is adopting a different approach to serving the community. She aims to disrupt the traditional museum focus that puts objects and buildings first, before people. To Garcia, building a "sense of place," by reprioritizing people and their stories and giving objects the supporting role, is crucial to disrupting the flow.[11]

A recent (2021) ASU Art Museum exhibition *Undoing Time: Art and the Histories of Incarceration* presented work that shifted penitentiary perspectives that focused on the East Coast to those that featured the Southwest, such as the incarceration of Indigenous people and Japanese Americans. To frame the exhibition, the museum linked twelve artists with activist organizations working to end mass incarceration, including Mass Liberation Arizona and the Arizona Interfaith Network, which, among other issues, organizes to end mass incarceration. Their collaboration included community-led site visits to reflect on the history of incarceration in Arizona. Garcia said, "Working with community activists completely changed our methodology. . . . It taught us a lot about how we think about audiences."[12] It shifted the orientation not only of the museum but also of the artists and community organizers with whom they worked, informing their role as storytellers.

Museums also offer conventional community services. The Fitchburg Art Museum, in Worcester County, Massachusetts, provided pandemic relief to the surrounding areas, including food and supplies for families and schools in 2022. The Crystal Bridges Museum of American Art, in Bentonville, Arkansas, commissioned nine local artists to create murals they brought to hospitals, senior living facilities, and isolated populations to relieve loneliness in 2020. And the Museum of Latin American Art, in Long Beach, California, serves as a voting site and offers voter registration services. They also run legal clinics around immigration and housing and provide space to health care providers for public health services, addressing medical issues ranging from COVID-19 to diabetes.

These community-based approaches to service and advocacy represent ways museums deepen public trust, engage community organizations, and support the cultural work of local institutions.. When their interests align, the impact of their work may be more widely felt.

How a Museum Inspires Community Activism

Museum exhibitions and programs have the capacity to influence ideas that shape political conflict. Some museums create a narrative picture of life based around different stories and themes, such as the Tenement Museum, in New York City, which depicts the lives of immigrants, the Holocaust museums in Israel, Germany, Washington, DC, and elsewhere, and the Apartheid Museum in Johannesburg, South Africa. It's impossible to escape their emotional impact on our beliefs and ideas.

Although they reach a narrow slice of the public, museums

nevertheless draw millions of people to their shows annually, and museum audiences believe the information gleaned from their experience is reliable, even more so than information they receive from nongovernmental organizations (NGOs) or newspapers.[13] So the possibility to shape popular views through curatorial decisions operates at a meaningful scale. That's reason enough for community organizations to think strategically about how they might work with or challenge museum programs, exhibitions, and labor practices.

The Legacy Museum and the National Memorial for Peace and Justice, in Montgomery, Alabama, demonstrate just how influential cultural institutions can be in their portrayal of contemporary and historical movements, in a way that links the past with current community interests and creates space to imagine what the future might hold.

In 2018, tapping a mix of legal advocates, organizers, artists, designers, funders, and architects, Bryan Stevenson, attorney and bestselling author of *Just Mercy*, founded these two important cultural spaces under the umbrella of the Equal Justice Initiative (EJI). Stevenson founded EJI in 1989 to provide legal assistance to innocent death row prisoners, to confront abuse of the incarcerated and the mentally ill, and to aid children prosecuted as adults. In keeping with his view that "justice movements have been sustained by artists," the museum and memorial shed light on the history of white supremacy and work to shift the many inaccurate but dominant narratives that have been promoted by white supremacists to justify their actions.[14] A basic tenet of EJI is that our ability to redress racial injustice is contingent on our ability to unravel the belief systems that have kept it in place.

Stevenson conceived of these spaces as public sites of memory, where families can begin to heal and take comfort in their remembrances and where they can partner with local communities to spur racial justice organizing.

Situated near one of the most active slave auction sites in America, the Legacy Museum traces the history of white supremacy from enslavement through mass incarceration, providing a powerful and sobering immersive experience.

Multimedia presentations and exhibitions fill the 11,000-square-foot museum.

Renowned African American visual artists, including Titus Kaphar, Glenn Ligon, and Jacob Lawrence, inspire reflection on our history. Two hundred installations lining the pathways throughout the museum bring the viewer into a state of quiet alarm. Holograms and interactive technology draw the observer more deeply into the lives of the enslaved and incarcerated. In one installation designed like a prison visitation room, the visitor sits and lifts a phone to speak with the prisoner behind the glass. The visitor is jolted when the life-like hologram projected on the other side of the glass lifts their own phone and speaks of his or her incarceration experience. In another installation, ghostlike holographic replicas of enslaved people, positioned within narrow confines, tell their family story when viewers approach.

The museum's narrative arc, connecting the slave trade to the era of Reconstruction, to lynching and Jim Crow laws, and then to mass incarceration, leaves nothing to the imagination. The sheer brutality forces the viewer to confront racialized terror. In this way, the museum reframes American history, replacing white artist–driven and curator–driven narratives with the legacy of racial inequality, truth, and reconciliation that leads to real solutions to contemporary problems in this country. It makes a significant departure from the tradition of most museums that have excluded broad cultural representation from their boardrooms, leadership positions, exhibitions, and collections.

The power of the exhibitions compels viewers to ask what can be done. And it is precisely the question of "what can be done" that separates the Legacy Museum and the National Memorial for Peace and Justice from many other cultural spaces. They not only reframe our public histories, but also inspire action by linking their narrative work and art to local racial justice organizing across the nation.

Through its Community Remembrance Project, the Equal Justice Initiative connects community residents from towns and counties where their ancestors were lynched by white supremacists. To aid community organizing, museum staff developed an organizer's toolkit, a step-by-step guide for community activists and organizations that focuses on researching past lynchings. They determine which groups have historically worked together to promote racial justice and develop a plan with them and other members of the community for healing, remembrances, and policy change.

This work is grounded in the belief that without sites of historical memory, we are doomed as a nation to forget our history. EJI attorney Sia Sanneh put it this way: "It is our hope that by telling the history of the African American experience in this country we expose the narratives that have allowed us as a country to tolerate suffering and injustice among people of color."[15]

Blocks away from the museum, the National Memorial for Peace and Justice brings lynching into sharp relief. Eight hundred and five six-foot-long weathered and rusted Corten steel beams hang to memorialize documented victims of racial violence in the United States, each etched with the victim's name and location of their lynching.[16] *New York Times* writer Campbell Robertson described the powerful hillside memorial as a "name by name reckoning . . .

dedicated to the victims of white supremacy and the lynching of Black people."[17] *See Plate 9.*

Through the Remembrance Project, local alliances gather their communities and deploy a wide array of art to dramatize their history by linking artists and their work with advocate organizations. Songs, spoken word performances, film and documentary screenings, oral

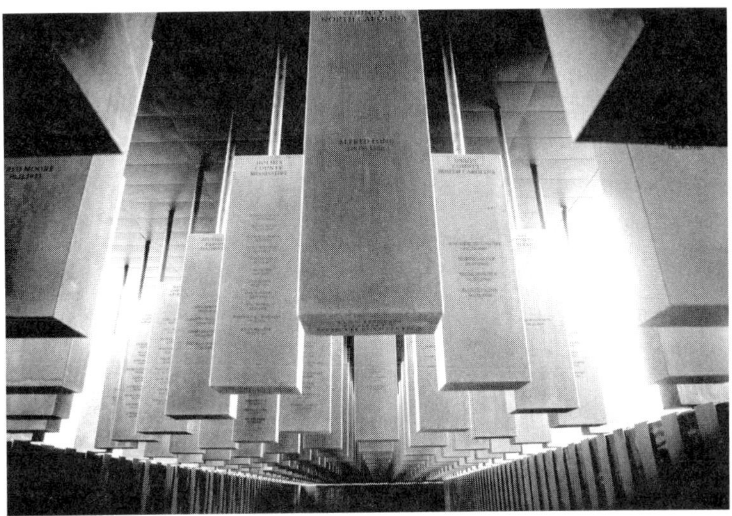

Partial view of the National Memorial for Peace and Justice in Montgomery, Alabama. Eight hundred and five six-foot-long hanging Corten steel monuments are dedicated to the legacy of enslaved Black people terrorized by lynching. Photo courtesy of Equal Justice Initiative/Human Pictures.

> *For the hanged and beaten.*
> *For the shot, drowned, and burned.*
> *For the tortured, tormented, and terrorized.*
> *For those abandoned by the rule of law.*
> *We will remember.*
> *With hope because hopelessness is the enemy of justice.*
> *With courage because peace requires bravery.*
> *With persistence because justice is a constant struggle.*
> *With faith because we shall overcome.*
> EJI-authored

history projects, local exhibitions, and community vigils strengthen the community bonds that animate their efforts.

Soil collection ceremonies have been a powerful means to reflect on the past. Hundreds of jars of soil from lynching sites across America are on display in the Legacy Museum and now in local communities. In Athens, Georgia, three hundred people gathered for a soil collection ceremony.

Other communities participate in historical marker initiatives to memorialize those lynched in the public square, sparking legal and policy changes to existing law. In Colorado, the Denver-based Remembrance Project partnered with elected officials and community organizations to remove language from the state constitution that made slavery illegal "except as punishment" for a crime. The Maryland Lynching Memorial Project worked with Republican governor Larry Hogan to sign HB 307 into law, which created a statewide Truth and Reconciliation Commission for the purposes of developing a public education project and to "consider reparatory efforts."

EJI's far-reaching program offers educators a lesson plan to teach students about this history and a racial justice essay contest to encourage students to think more deeply about it.

These museum-inspired initiatives have one primary aim in common with community organizations: they all move people into action. That's the essence of organizing—people acting together in support of their values.

By highlighting the clear intersection between cultural landmarks and community organizing, EJI offers a model for museums to embed themselves more deeply in their communities. Their work also offers community organizers another glimpse of the role and impact of culture in building community and confronting oppression.

Inside and Outside Strategies for Change

Cultural institutions historically have been at least one step removed from conventional organizing and activism. The experience of the Legacy and Queens museums, and a growing number of similar examples, suggest this may be changing. But museums may be constrained from acting more quickly, partly because of past policy driven by a subset of conservative donors and board members and "art for art's sake" proponents. Often, their interests slant toward "museum neutrality"—which is to say they want museum exhibitions to be ahistorical on issues related to ideology, race, ethnicity, and culture and to stay clear of hot button issues like climate change and voter suppression. Instead, they advance the notion of maintaining a "proper distance," by which they mean they do not want museums to partner with community organizations that might advocate for or against issues.

Museum boards, like many nonprofit boards, tend to be filled by people who have wealth, power, and connections to other potential donors and community leaders. According to the latest survey of museum board membership (2017), 46 percent of museum boards are all white.[18]

These governing bodies include some of the richest people in the world, and whether they skew politically left or right, their elite status in society reflects an orientation to the world that differs from that of individuals without the same power, prestige, and privilege. Not until recent racial justice uprisings have museums been compelled to more intentionally recruit board members and staff who represent Main Street and come from different walks of life, from artists to organizers.

According to former Santa Cruz Museum of Art and History director Nina Simon,

> For a museum to survive and thrive today, it must be relevant and meaningful for many people from many backgrounds. It must sway to the pulse of the cultural community in which it resides. It must be radically inclusive, constantly working to invite new people to connect for new reasons.[19]

Activists are taking up this challenge by developing collaborative strategies with museum staff, who mostly trend liberal, and community and labor organizations, scientists, and others to challenge museum labor practices and boards that are stuck in a nineteenth- and twentieth-century frame of mind. They are stepping into a moment when museums are in flux, transforming their practices or resisting change on a range of issues, from making retrograde endowment investments to trying to eliminate "art washing," a term that refers to museum donors who use their philanthropic largesse to cover up or offset public perceptions of corporate malfeasance and practices that harm community.

Organizing from the Outside In

Some activists are positioning themselves as both advocates and antagonists, working with and in support of museum staff when possible or challenging a museum's slant when their exhibitions incorrectly portray or omit history that bears on such issues as climate change.

Not An Alternative, an art collective that works for climate and environmental justice, took one such step by organizing high-profile campaigns to drive gas and oil tycoon David Koch and billionaire Rebekah Mercer from the board of the American Museum of Natural History. Not An Alternative's co-founders Beka Economopoulos, environmental activist and organizer, and her partner Jason Jones, artist and exhibition designer, argued that putting funders of "science denial" in leadership positions was damaging to the museum's reputation as one of the most "revered and influential" science institutions in the world and was incongruous with its mission to "discover, interpret, and disseminate—through scientific research and education—knowledge about human cultures, the natural world, and the universe."[20]

Koch and Mercer exemplify many conservative scions of wealth who may have a vested interest in positioning cultural institutions, in this case science and history museums, as neutral venues that rise above the political fray. Although they make no bones about their interests in fossil fuels and climate change denial, they can publicly cloak their influence over museum exhibitions by arguing either explicitly or implicitly for museum neutrality. This throws a monkey wrench into museum operations.

As a result, curators in science and history museums, for instance, who grapple with developing meaningful exhibitions that illustrate how fossil fuel production contributes to rising earth temperatures are likely to proceed more cautiously. A former director of the Carnegie Museum of Natural History, in Pittsburgh, said that he could not talk directly about fossil fuels because many of his board members and donors made their wealth from them.[21]

In her recent book *Culture Strike: Art and Museums in an Age of Protest*, Laura Raicovich argues that

> the problem with neutrality as a claim for a museum is that it fundamentally neutralizes criticism, dissent or alternative history that it might present, which contradicts its very claim to free and open exchanges of ideas.[22]

It is not just their "neutrality" argument that is in play. When museum directors and curators decide on exhibitions, they often do so knowing which of their board members or benefactors might enjoy or be politically offended by their choices. As board members Koch and Mercer must have known, without saying a word, their presence alone ensured that museum staff would at least take their views into account.

Polls show that most museum visitors trust information they derive from their visits. So when climate deniers sit on the boards of natural history and science museums, their opinions may influence what information the trusting public receives. Ultimately, their presence can undermine the credibility of the institution and lead to questions about whether facts are being twisted or omitted in such a way as to spread misinformation.

To fuel protest over the role of these donors, Economopoulos considered her options, saying, "We could bike lock ourselves to the entrance of the American Museum of Natural History, but that was not going to win us any favors, or really supporters, because people walking through the door are already on our side and most of the staff probably as well."[23]

Instead, Not An Alternative adopted an organizing model: they mapped constituencies that could exert pressure on the museum to remove Koch and Mercer from the board and created a strategic alliance of artists, advocates, and, critically important, scientists to drive the campaign. Together they choreographed inside and outside strategies: working quietly with museum staff, sometimes on late-evening calls, to determine points of leverage, while climate change activists protested on the streets outside.

To build its campaigns against Koch (2015) and Mercer (2018), Not An Alternative distributed two letters from 150 to 200 of the world's top scientists and Nobel Prize laureates calling on museums to cut all ties to funders of climate science misinformation. These letters quickly went viral, laying the predicate for a petition campaign that generated 550,000 signatures to support their call for removal. After an avalanche of press, petition signatures, and op-eds, Koch stepped down from the board, after serving over twenty years. Though only he will know the exact reason he stepped down, it appeared to activists that there was an agreement among board leaders and Koch, and later Mercer, that maintaining a board slot would be too much trouble, and that it was a good time to part ways.[24]

This type of work aligns with the work of UK artist collective BP or not BP?, which pushed the London-based Tate Museums and the Royal Shakespeare Company to drop British Petroleum (BP) as a sponsor, and the Divest-Invest campaign spurred by the Wallace Global Fund to press foundations to divest their portfolios from fossil fuels and to invest in climate solutions. The crowning achievement of this campaign was persuading the Rockefeller Foundation, whose endowment comes from fossil fuels, to divest their own portfolios, opening the floodgates to other institutional and individual donors that followed suit. All told, as many as 170 investors divested $40 trillion as of October 2021.[25] And still counting.

If the Rockefellers could divest, there was reason for the activist art collective to believe that natural history and science museums across the country could be persuaded to do the same. In collaboration with 350.org, an international environmental movement organization working to end the use of fossil fuels and to support the use of renewable energy, a museum divestment movement was born. Though it will take time (not that we have any to spare), museums have started to divest their endowments from fossil fuels and to drop fossil fuel sponsors. In 2016, the American Museum of Natural History, in New York, held no direct investments in fossil fuel companies.[26] A number of other museums affiliated with the American Alliance of Museums, including the Field Museum of Chicago, the California Academy of Sciences in San Francisco, the Leonardo

Museum in Utah, and the Phipps Conservatory and Botanical Garden in Pittsburgh, announced they had divested or were in the process of divesting.[27] An organization called Upstart Co-Lab, an impact investing company, is working with museums to proactively invest their endowment in low-income communities.

While activists, such as those connected to Not An Alternative, are challenging museum practices that contribute to climate change and denial, other activists are driving campaigns against art washing. This kind of "philanthropy" was publicly exposed on a large scale by the campaigns against the Sackler family, owner of Purdue Pharma, the company that fueled the opioid crisis with the highly addictive painkiller OxyContin. The CDC reports that nearly five hundred thousand Americans died from opioid overdoses between 1999 and 2019.[28]

The Sacklers invested deeply in the art world, including cultural institutions in China, the United States, and Europe. In an exposé for the *Washington Post*, Peggy McGlone revealed that the family donated one thousand works of art, with an estimated value of $50 million, to the Smithsonian, plus $4 million to store the collection. Jillian Sackler, following the death of her husband Arthur, donated another $6 million to the national institution.[29] This sum of $60 million reflects just one of dozens of national and international contributions the Sackler family foundations have made. Contributions at this scale build influence. If the Sacklers, or other donors of a similar status, threatened to withhold their funds, some museums, as they operate today, could be crippled and forced to reckon with their priorities.

In connection with ongoing litigation seeking restitution for their role in pushing highly addictive drugs, New York attorney general Letitia James said the Sackler family "used their ill-gotten wealth to cover-up their misconduct with a philanthropic campaign intending to whitewash their decades-long success."[30] Patrick Radden Keefe, author of *Empire of Pain*, put it like this: "[The] Sacklers gave money to fancy institutions . . . cultivating their reputation as big philanthropists. The whole family was kind of relentlessly branding themselves. . . . At the Tate Museum in London, you can [even] ride the Sackler elevator."[31]

Photographer-activist Nan Goldin, who became addicted to OxyContin during the opioid crisis, founded P.A.I.N. (Prescription Addiction Intervention Now) to inspire an activist art movement to sever Sackler links with museums. The campaign called on cultural institutions to shed Sackler funding and remove the Sackler name from their rooms, walls, and lists of contributors.

A snowstorm of prescriptions fluttered through the lobby of New York's Guggenheim Museum, scattered by hundreds of artists and activists, while other participants dropped to the floor in a "die-in" protest. A few blocks away, at the Metropolitan Museum of Art,

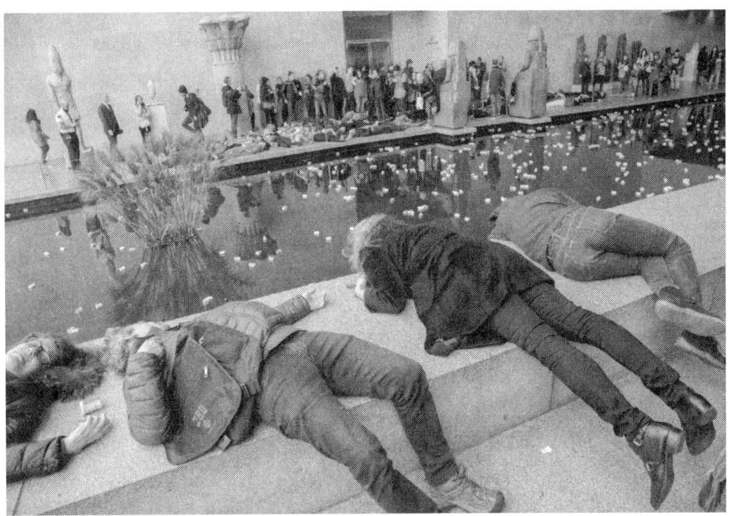

Inspired by Nan Goldin, this "die-in" dramatized activists' demands to remove the Sackler name from the Met and other cultural institutions. Photo © JC Barcourt/Sackler P.A.I.N.

Goldin organized one hundred demonstrators to throw pill bottles marked "prescribed to you by the Sackler family" into the moat around the Temple of Dendur.

Soon thereafter, as the vast number of OxyContin-related addictions and deaths became more publicly visible, aided in part by pending litigation against Purdue Pharma and the Sackler family, the Metropolitan Museum of Art, the Tate and other British museums, and the Louvre, in Paris, wiped away mention of the Sackler name from their buildings and gallery spaces, including the wing of the Met that houses the Temple of Dendur.[32] As of December 2021, the American Museum of Natural History, Tate Modern in London, and the Jewish Museum Berlin also pledged not to take Sackler funds.

There has always been and will always be robber barons who use their largesse to burnish their reputations. Their presence in leadership positions and their use of funding to influence decision-making have always raised questions as to what responsibility museums (and other institutions) have to the public. Many museums rely on this support for their work, but they have yet to systematically grapple with these issues. Instead, museum leaders weigh the intensity of community pressure against their financial interests. When communities and cultural workers exert enough pressure on donors and board members, as they did in different ways with Koch, Mercer, and the Sackler family, their organizing makes change possible.

When Community Leaders, Artists, and Museums Collaborate

While some activists target museums for social action, there are growing signs that museums are strategically partnering with community activists and organizations to leverage the impact art bears on current events. The Speed Art Museum, in Louisville, Kentucky, offers a model for best practice and demonstrates how these partnerships can heal and build community, and for how museums can facilitate connections.

Louisville is the home to the Kentucky Derby, mint juleps, Muhammad Ali, and the Louisville Slugger, a highly sought-after baseball bat. It also has a deeply racist past, which continues to find expression through the state song and unofficial Kentucky Derby anthem, Stephen Foster's "My Old Kentucky Home." Previously sung at minstrel shows by performers in blackface, it is still sung annually at Churchill Downs.[33]

In 2020, Breonna Taylor, a Louisville-based twenty-six-year-old Black woman and medical worker, was shot in her apartment by white police officers. Taylor's killing shattered the community and the nation. That year, the derby modified its presentation, and the lyrics went unsung—but it still sanctioned a single bugle player to perform "My Old Kentucky Home."[34]

It was in response to this cultural climate that the Speed Art Museum found itself thrown into the heart of the BLM movement. Four years earlier, it had completed a major four-year renovation that transformed the museum, in the words of former museum board chair Martha Slaughter, "from an inward facing windowless repository for the collection and scholarly exhibitions, to an outward facing transparent glass box."[35] Unlike their daunting 1927 galleries of marble and travertine, the new building invited Louisville residents in. Sadiqa Reynolds, CEO of the Louisville Urban League, echoed this sentiment, saying, "Prior to the renovation, the community perception was that it wasn't a place for the community. It felt very closed off."[36]

The museum picked up on work done by a former museum director, Peter Morrin, who in the 1990s created a kind of a community advisory board that, ahead of its time, represented forward movement toward inclusion and helped to connect the museum directly with artist Sam Gilliam.[37] After Morrin left, the advisory board lay dormant for more than a decade.

In response to Breonna Taylor's death, museum director Stephen Reily asked himself what it meant to serve the community at a time of trial. His question spoke to street protests and the racial justice reckoning taking place across the nation while white police officers in Minnesota were standing trial for the murder of George Floyd.

Rapid response to contemporary events has never been museums' forte. It's almost an oxymoron. Exhibitions are planned years in advance. It takes time to strike agreements to borrow work from art collectors and other museums, and exhibition planning often involves consultation with a wide range of stakeholders, often funders and curators and, infrequently, with community activists and organizations.

If the Speed wanted to respond to the cultural moment happening in its own backyard, it had to pivot quickly. And pivot the Speed did. In just four months, the museum emptied five of its primary galleries and created a critically acclaimed exhibition entitled *Promise, Witness, Remembrance*, centering the life, death, and legacy of Breonna Taylor.

The centerpiece of the exhibition was a portrait of Taylor painted by artist Amy Sherald, who had painted the official portrait of First Lady Michelle Obama, which hangs in the Smithsonian National Portrait Gallery. Writer and commentator Ta-Nehisi Coates commissioned Taylor's portrait for *Vanity Fair*'s special edition on activism, and Sherald wanted it seen by people in Louisville. Sherald said,

> I knew in my gut that it should be in her hometown as a balm in Gilead. That the museum space could become a place to process, soothe and heal. A place of reflection and quiet. . . . I wanted to create something that would assist in codifying the moment and the movement.[38] *See Plate 10.*

In a story featuring the exhibition, *New York Times* art critic Holland Cotter wrote,

> The history that our big, general-interest art museums promote, through their preservation and display of objects, is primarily a white history, with views of all other histories filtered through it. But that slanted perspective is no longer representative of audiences that museums will—speaking purely pragmatically—need to attract to survive.[39]

The museum's leadership understood that inclusive practices in developing the exhibition would be necessary to help the Louisville community come together, and they positioned the exhibition as a catalyst for change.

Meeting with Tamika Palmer, Breonna Taylor's mother, was step one. The museum would not create the exhibition without Ms. Palmer's approval; as Reily said, "Our view was that Ms. Palmer had veto rights." Palmer's thoughts about her daughter's death shaped the themes of the show. She, along with her family, helped conceive the path forward and became a driving force for the development of the exhibition and for the partnerships between the museum and the community.

The process included creating two essential advisory boards. One was a national advisory panel made up of artists and people affected by police brutality and gun violence. Organized by curator Allison Glenn, it included artist Theaster Gates, who had worked with the Tamir Rice Foundation; photographer Hank Willis Thomas, whose cousin was violently killed; Raymond Green, a cousin to Alton Sterling, whom police killed in Baton Rouge, Louisiana; and La Keisha Leek, a cousin to Trayvon Martin. Together with Glenn, they helped frame the exhibition.

The second committee, a local advisory board, was composed of mental health experts, civil rights attorneys, local protest and civic leaders, and two board members, who would ensure that whatever process was created to develop the exhibition would not be "one and done" but would have legs beyond the exhibition.

The local advisory board insisted on several items. They wanted all the artists in the exhibition to be Black artists. They wanted more local artists, not just national figures. And given that Breonna's life was vibrant and upbeat, they wanted the exhibition to be colorful. That last point was also reflected in Sherald's portrait, which shows Breonna in a turquoise dress.

Some demands of the local committee were at odds with the national committee and the curator, but ultimately Glenn and the museum prioritized the local relationships. Rather than approach the exhibition with the view that curatorial expertise would reign, Toya Northington, a former social worker who served as the museum's community engagement strategist, said the exhibition was "built on conversations about how a museum could get it right, how the art world would respond, and what it meant to collaborate in this [social justice] space."[40]

Board chair Martha Slaughter said people came to the museum who probably would never step inside a museum otherwise. In planning for the exhibition and following it, the community recognized the museum wanted to be part of their lives.

The process the museum undertook to build the exhibition, guided by Breonna Taylor's family and local and national figures, many from outside of the museum world, created new alliances. *New York Times* writer Siddhartha Mitter wrote that because of the committees, the museum could "avoid the shoals on which museums have foundered in their effort to address trauma and inequity in their communities and in their own practice."[41]

The thirty-piece exhibition included artists Sam Gilliam and Glenn Ligon; photographer Jon P. Cherry, who documented the street protest in Louisville; and video artist Jon-Sesrie Goff, whose four-minute video reflects the aftermath of the 2015 mass shooting at Emanuel AME Church in Charleston, South Carolina. The exhibition was supplemented by film and panel discussions. During the COVID-19 pandemic, the museum provided a safe place for community organizations to meet, becoming something of a hub, a center reflecting the title of the exhibition *Promise, Witness, Remembrance.*

The advance work leading up to the exhibition and the exhibition itself transformed how the museum operates and relates to the community. It's planning timeline, or the exhibition runway as it is called, shifted from a three-to-five-year process to one of four months, suggesting that the museum can effectively respond to future current events.

By consulting directly with Tamika Palmer and her family and by creating the local and national advisory committees to inform the show, the community became integral and authentic participants in the exhibition design and message. Reily said they felt invested in the process and in the institution. Louisville's Black community could trust, at least more than they have in the past, that the museum would present art relevant to their lives, including such basic services as offering space for community meetings in the newly redesigned museum. The process demonstrates that community leaders and organizers can creatively shape a museum's role and influence and suggests they can leverage a museum's influence to support the community.

Communities of color represent roughly 23 percent of the Louisville population. Staff sensitivity to the racial, local, and national political dynamics—particularly in an intense period of racial uprising—reflected the best of inclusive practices and made Kentucky's oldest museum a more vibrant cultural center.

A Renewed Push for Equity

Though not without historical precedent, against the backdrop of the coronavirus pandemic and the movement for Black lives, there was a sharp uptick in union organizing among some of the four hundred thousand–plus museum workers in the United States. The exact number of workers who are participating in these drives is difficult to pinpoint as many unionization campaigns are underway now, some public and some not.

That said, by the end of 2020, workers in more than two dozen art museums had voted to join a range of unions. The United Museum Workers and the Carnegie museums in Pittsburgh joined the United Steelworkers. Workers at the Minneapolis Walker Art Center joined the American Federation of State, County and Municipal Employees (AFSCME), one of two primary unions that organize cultural workers. At the Milwaukee Art Museum, staff voted to join the Machinists Union (IAM). Employees at the Museum of Fine Arts (MFA) in Boston, Massachusetts, joined the United Auto Workers (UAW), which represents cultural workers at some fifteen major museums, from the Museum of Modern Art to the Whitney Museum, primarily on the East Coast.[42]

Not surprisingly, these organizing campaigns revolve around job security, compensation, and racial justice. The pandemic spurred unionization efforts in what now appear to be obvious ways. Museums were shut down. Workers were furloughed and felt the sense of powerlessness that drives much of union organizing. The organizing campaigns validated their experience as they sought leverage to protect themselves.

A trigger to the current wave of organizing was the "Arts + All Museums Salary Transparency," a spreadsheet posted anonymously online in 2019, which compared self-reported worker salaries across museums as they relate to executive compensation.[43] Workers from different museums could add their own salaries by institution, an interactive process that connected them to one another. The income inequality was dramatic—and the spreadsheet went viral. Sheila Majumdar, an organizer at the Art Institute of Chicago, said, "We want equity baked into our contract."[44] Tom Juravich, a professor at the University of Massachusetts Amherst, said, "They [cultural workers] realized they were being treated more like servants to the elite."[45]

Like organizing in any industry, the wave of unionization in museums stems from workers who feel vulnerable to market whims. They are concerned about future employment and poor compensation and seek a larger voice in policy decisions that govern their work. While cultural workers in the performing arts have long been unionized, such as stagehands, actors, dancers, and operating engineers, those in museums have had a more difficult run. Many of these workers, such as museum guards, are paid low wages, some as low at $15 to $20 hourly. Maida Rosenstein, a former art student who started organizing museum workers more than forty years ago and who until recently served as president of the United Auto Workers Local 2110, said more than half of their union members who work at the Whitney Museum earn less than $20 hourly. This contrasts with the pay of the Museum of Modern Art's director, Glenn Lowry, who received more than $2.2 million in salary, bonuses, and benefits in fiscal year 2017.[46] It's the kind of income inequality that drove the Occupy movement and drives other campaigns across economic sectors.

This internal economic imbalance is exacerbated further by museums' extensive use of part-time workers, which enables them to avoid the costs of paying full benefits. Many museum educators are adjuncts who are paid a per diem wage. Art handlers, who install and de-install exhibitions and at times undertake potentially dangerous job assignments, work mostly part-time.

The arguments to maintain a low-wage and part-time workforce in cultural institutions are not dissimilar to those made by nonprofits, who claim they don't have enough grant dollars to support a living wage. Maybe yes and maybe no, but wealthy donors serve on many museum boards and contribute large sums, especially to support art exhibitions they love. Museum holdings are often worth billions of dollars. Amidst the plenty, can equity be achieved?

Organizing among cultural workers has thus far tended to work in parallel with community activism. In discussing collaboration between unions and community activists, Rosenstein notes that their relationship is sometimes "complicated" because museum workers can view protesters as "outsiders" when activists demanding change pressure museum staff to make changes. Complicating things further, museum trustees have relationships with museum workers, especially curators, whose work they fund. In some cases, their largesse—much to their credit—helped workers through the pandemic when they donated to worker funds or supported bonuses for workers, strengthening their relationship with the workforce.

These dynamics represent challenges inherent in museum culture and will affect the extent of collaboration between unionized cultural workers, nonprofit organizations, and other community activists who share common goals. But the growing number of unions at these cultural sites suggests, as history reflects, that community and labor collaboration may be in the making.

And while no "formal" collaboration between unions and activists has yet to materialize, museum workers have joined in and have sometimes led community campaigns, such as at the Whitney in 2019, when more than one hundred workers signed a letter to museum leaders denouncing board vice chair Warren Kanders, CEO of Kanders and Company, whose affiliate bought Safariland, LLC, which manufactured the tear gas U.S. border patrol agents used against immigrants on the border during the Trump administration.

An internal staff memo, originally a response to an article about Kanders in the online art journal *Hyperallergic*, was leaked to the media and helped generate a protracted eight-month firestorm over his leadership. Public protest followed and social media lit up. The artist and activist collective Decolonize This Place helped build the

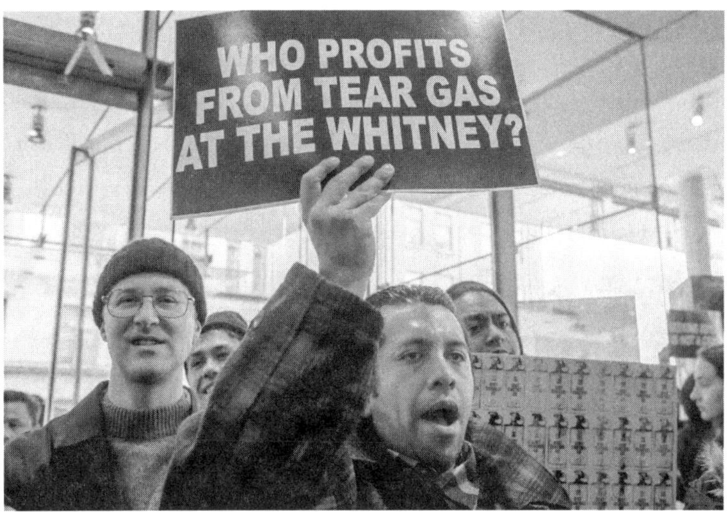

Museum workers and community allies call on the Whitney to oust board vice chair Warren Kanders, CEO of Safariland, the company that produced the tear gas used by law enforcement officials to suppress protesters on the U.S.-Mexico border. Photo © Erik McGregor/Pacific Press/Alamy Live News.

campaign against Kanders, bringing protesters to the museum day in and day out. Several artists withdrew from the Whitney Biennial in protest, while others passed around anti–tear gas stickers. Kanders resigned.

To respond to a moment in which America's institutions are grappling with their fraught past, from slavery to economic inequality, dozens of new projects between museums and community organizations are developing.

The work of cultural institutions that are focused on community building, the wave of unionization and protests demanding fair labor practices, and the demands of activists for museums to end the charade of museum neutrality and art washing are also signs of change in the air.

Social justice organizers and cultural workers will step up and push museums to go further, just as museums will increasingly embrace a more strategic approach to tackling long-standing concerns pivoting around race, class, and gender. As the Queens, Legacy, and Speed Museums demonstrate, these new collaborations with labor and community organizations may enable each to garner new resources that support the "common good." Fundamentally, they will drive engagement with civil society and contemporary issues, rather than be isolated individual experiences only—an essential step to catalyzing change.

6

Toward Art, Activism, and Transformative Philanthropy

Charity is no substitute for justice.

—Michael Eric Dyson[1]

In 1976, philanthropist and art collector Agnes Gund, "Aggie" to all who know her, purchased pop artist Roy Lichtenstein's *Masterpiece* (1962), a comic strip caricature of a couple fawning over a painting, calling *Masterpiece* a "masterpiece." *See Plate 3.* Aggie, who became close friends with Roy and his wife Dorothy, hung *Masterpiece* in the living room of her Upper East Side home in New York City.

Decades later, after watching Ava DuVernay's documentary film *13th* (2016), which painfully traces the history of slavery to mass incarceration, Aggie was inspired to invest in criminal justice system reform and contacted longtime friend and colleague Darren Walker, president of the Ford Foundation, to ask what they could do together.

The film and that fateful discussion prompted another conversation, this time with Dorothy Lichtenstein, who was enthusiastic about the prospect of Aggie selling *Masterpiece* to raise funds to end mass incarceration. Aggie's daughter, Emmy-nominated filmmaker Catherine Gund, who said her mother is driven by relationships, suggested that her decision to sell Lichtenstein's *Masterpiece* was a "way in which she was also honoring Dorothy."[2] In June 2017, it was reported that Aggie donated $100 million of the proceeds from that sale to create the Art for Justice Fund (A4J).[3]

The Gund family story and other philanthropic initiatives discussed in the following pages reflect how new thinking and new sources of philanthropy are changing funding patterns and practices, just as they're altering how art and advocate organizations do their work. Their approach to social change serves as a blueprint for philanthropy that, to paraphrase the Ford Foundation's Walker, is inspired by philanthropy moving from generosity to justice.[4]

From Tangled Roots

The art and social justice field within philanthropy is relatively new. In the early twentieth century, "cultural philanthropy" ignored art for social movements and virtually excluded communities of color from receiving charitable donations. In her report *Fusing Arts, Culture and Social Change*, prepared for the National Committee for Responsive Philanthropy (NCRP), Holly Sidford notes,

> For the most part, early cultural philanthropy did not support the democratic artwork of the settlement houses or pay attention to the arts and culture of Native American peoples, African Americans, or immigrants' groups from China, Europe, and other parts of the world.[5]

Early cultural philanthropy funded the building of elite art institutions and the commissioning and acquiring of high-end art in a market where gallerists and museum curators were the predominant voices in defining value. Funding for the arts became the domain of mostly white male philanthropists. It neither reflected community interests nor lifted community aspirations. It stood apart from day-to-day life, positioned "above the fray." To this moment, we can see the vestiges of old cultural philanthropy continue to play out in the debate over whether museums and galleries are "neutral spaces" or whether they prioritize one set of ideas and values above others.

Hence, it's no surprise there remains a litany of long-standing issues confronting "art for social change" funders, not the least of which are those related to race, class, and gender. And there exists no shortage of critique among grant recipients, academics, community organizations, and funders themselves over the political and policy impact of their funding practices. Reformers on the left, like the NCRP, have long sought to change and democratize funding patterns and practices.

Unlike elite art and cultural institutions, most of the circumstances and factors that ignite social movements have little or nothing to do with institutionalized philanthropy. In Occupy Wall Street and the Movement for Black Lives, for example, art and organizing received little upfront foundation support.[6] It was growing economic inequality, the 99% versus the 1%, that triggered Occupy, and it was white police killings of African Americans that triggered the new movement for Black lives. Both were made visible by labor and community organizing and by spontaneous expressions of art, from murals, videos, comedy, and posters to music and spoken word.

Nonetheless, organizers and artists need money to scale and sustain their work. Philanthropy offers or withholds potentially catalytic support. Staff can be hired, communications and field operations developed, and new strategic initiatives launched. In the context of art for social justice, when all three players—artists, organizers, and funders—share common interests, and when trust between them develops, their overlapping work becomes more entwined, these partnerships deepen, and all three increase their capacity to reach their goals. Cliff Albright of the Black Voters Matter Capacity Building Institute calls these relationships "the infrastructure of power-building."[7]

Precedent-Setting Initiatives

Dating back to the 1960s to the 1990s, foundations like Rockefeller, Ford, and Surdna were making large grants to social justice–oriented art projects and initiatives, but it wasn't until the early part of the twenty-first century that a field of practice within institutionalized philanthropy, systematically funding art for social justice, got underway.

Philanthropy has always had a small group of risk-takers, open to breaking away from conventional practice and willing to fund new strategies. Claudine Brown, the director of the art and culture program at the Nathan Cummings Foundation (Cummings) from 1995 to 2010, was a trailblazer. When it came to innovative philanthropic ideas that link art and community change, few foundations were more invested in supporting these practices than Cummings. The foundation had a social action agenda, animated by the family's Jewish tradition of Tikkun Olam (to repair the world).[8]

Brown's north star was her belief that art is among the world's greatest assets. The Cummings board supported Brown's work to fund initiatives that informed how artists, art organizations, and community organizations relate to each other to strengthen future collaborations. To learn how artists can deploy art for social change, she moved beyond what to organizers and funders was a crucial question: how to quantify the immediate impact of funding. Instead, Brown sought nontraditional, qualitative criteria to measure the impact of art, which differs from the metrics of organizing for a vote or passing legislation.

Her questions coursed their way through philanthropy, spawning new research and experiments that galvanized the funding community. In 2010, a handful of activist funders, including the Cross-Currents, Nathan Cummings, Lambent, Open Society, and Surdna

Foundations, jointly commissioned the Animating Democracy program at Americans for the Arts, to develop an arts and social change mapping initiative they called *Trend or Tipping Point: Arts and Social Change Grantmaking.*[9] It was the first methodical mapping of institutional philanthropy that highlighted the challenges to funding art and culture in social change circles while also profiling different strategic approaches. It gave visibility to the foundations and community organizations without which social change philanthropy would be meaningless.

Prior to this report, there had been no common language among funders to describe this shift within institutional philanthropy, nor did these funders share a common language with organizers. Michelle Coffey, executive director of the Lambent Foundation, said Animating Democracy offered "a vernacular that had not yet been present."[10]

To present their findings, the report's authors, Pam Korza and Barbara Schaffer Bacon, convened funders far and wide, highlighting their work in places that ranged from house meetings to foundation board rooms.

The report supplemented Brown's effort to establish a working group on art and social justice within the Grantmakers in the Arts (GIA), an umbrella organization of some three hundred foundations that support art and culture. A member of the GIA board, Brown hosted day-long preconference meetings on art and social change, using the GIA convenings as a primary vehicle to advance these new ideas. While she convened funders at Grantmaker meetings, Brown continued to connect foundation leaders with social justice practitioners and artists in meetings at the Cummings headquarters and elsewhere.

Much of this work was stewarded by women of color, including Brown, Regina Smith (former GIA board chair), Erlin Ibreck (Open

Society Foundation), Maurine Knighton (who was Brown's successor at Cummings), and Michelle Coffey. It was picked up by the National Committee for Responsive Philanthropy in its work to close the equity gap in grantmaking between white-led organizations and those within communities of color. Since 2017, under the leadership of president Eddie Torres, GIA has more methodically promoted the linkage between art and culture funders and social justice and has become a leading institutional voice within philanthropy to push foundations to support BIPOC leaders on the same scale white-led art and social change organizations are supported.

An Organizer, Artist, and Funder Combine Forces

Meanwhile, individual foundations, large and small, took initiative to demonstrate the value of funding at the intersection of art and social justice. The small (but nimble) family foundation CrossCurrents supported one such initiative.

In 2013, muralist Justin Nethercut, street name "Nether," and Carol Ott, a housing organizer, stepped into the fray of Baltimore's housing crisis. Baltimore is one of the few remaining East Coast cities where entire city blocks of homes sit vacant and uninhabitable. Nether and Ott wanted more people from outside these communities to take notice and to petition the city for a remedy.

Working with a team of artists, Nether wheat-pasted or painted fifteen murals on the walls of these vacant buildings. Each mural told a story about housing and slumlords and about Baltimore and dreams, those of the artists and the community. But it was not just vivid imagery and colorful art on desolate Baltimore streets that captured public attention. On each mural, Nether pasted a QR code that when scanned took viewers to a website that identified the building owners by name, along with their contact information and the names of elected officials in whose districts the buildings sat.

One mural featured a large purple-black-and-gold raven building a nest—wood slats gripped in its claws, caution tape hanging from its beak, symbolizing a determination to rebuild from the rubble. *See Plate 7.* The day after the artist, Stefan Ways, created it, Nether found the QR code ripped off the raven mural. After replacing the code, he then encountered demolition signs, and within weeks the building was torn down. The story reached the media. The headline of a local blog about the project read "Art Aimed to Shame" and an *ABC 2 News* headline read "Illegal Street Art Calls Out Owner of Baltimore's Vacant Properties."[11]

Political tension also heightened over a mural by the street artist Gaia that depicted the crown of King Tut with the visage replaced by a cotton field and the image of a suburban home with eagle wings floating above the word "exodus," written in in Hebrew and English. The mural was intended to visualize the connections between the Jewish and African American experiences with oppression and migration.

In response, the *Baltimore Sun* assigned three journalists to the story and reported that the landlord (as revealed through the QR code) denied owning the building.[12] In a counterattack, the landlord accused the artist of reinforcing the anti-Semitic notion that Jewish landlords keep Black communities down and took housing organizer Carol Ott, who did the research behind the QR codes, to court, but to no avail. Gaia, Nether, and Ott immediately challenged the denial of ownership and described the landlord's attack as politically motivated—designed to divert attention from his responsibilities for the building. According to the *City Paper*, a local weekly publication, this landlord was well known, having been "forced to mitigate lead-paint issues in more than 500 homes."[13]

The *City Paper* also challenged the landlord's claim, running a comprehensive story detailing its independent research that pointed to many strands of evidence strongly suggesting the property was under his control.[14] Shortly after the dustup over Gaia's mural, other murals rocked the city (which owned many of these vacant properties) and local realtors. The mayor responded to the political chaos the murals generated. A *Baltimore Sun* headline appeared: "City to Raze Hundreds of Vacant Houses in Stepped-Up Plan."[15] The article reported that the city had increased its $2.5 million demolition budget to $22 million to tear down 1,500 abandoned houses.

This much-abbreviated story, written up in the *Grantmakers in the Arts* quarterly edition and presented to the GIA board, illustrated to funders and others how a unique collaboration between a funder, an artist, a housing organizer, and the community could leverage their power to influence city officials.[16] Ed Fuentes, cultural writer and Latino art advocate, wrote, "From the words of poets to the streets of Skid Row . . . murals are still storytellers with some bite."[17]

Tapping Pop Culture

Building on a still-emerging philanthropic arts and social change field, a number of funders, including some who supported the *Trend and Tipping Point* report, looked toward narrative change and how cultural views might be shifted to align with and tell the true story of our history. In a 2009 paper advocating cultural recovery as part of the Obama administration's program for national recovery, writer, painter, and cultural activist Arlene Goldbard argued that "culture is an effective crucible for social transformation, one that can be less polarizing and create deeper connections than other social change arenas."[18]

After participating in discussions about the role of art in organizing and the impact of the work being done by her colleagues at the Nathan Cummings and Ford Foundations, Unbound Philanthropy, a foundation that focuses primarily on immigrant justice, began making discretionary grants for the arts. The foundation was eager to experiment with how to scale its work, and the arts offered an additional way to do it.

Executive director Taryn Higashi concluded these projects merited support, but by themselves they did not add up to the kind of change she and the community with which she worked sought. For one, the scale of impact was limited, and for another, the projects let stand inaccurate narratives about people, culture, and communities, including those narratives that fueled racist stereotypes in communities of colors, such as the immigrant community that Unbound worked to support.

In 2015, Unbound Philanthropy and the Nathan Cummings Foundation jointly commissioned the *#PopJustice* series, a six-part report prepared by Liz Mann Strategy "intended for funders and social justice advocates interested in the promise and potential of pop culture as an agent of change."[19]

In defining the impact of pop culture, Liz Mann argued that the entertainment industry, including film, music, comedy, and TV, and literary art forms, as well as "practices and pastimes," such as car racing, hunting, and faith-based practices, were essential behavioral drivers.[20] It is within this ocean of culture that strategies to influence ideas could make a difference of scale.

Nor was it just conjecture. While the *#PopJustice* volumes draw on empirical evidence, one needs only to have watched sitcoms like those created by Norman Lear, such as *All in the Family* and *The Jeffersons*, to see their impact. Millions of families viewed these TV shows in their homes, weekly episodes that took on bigotry and homophobia. They spoke to ordinary people who saw themselves in the characters the sitcoms created. Norman Lear would say "that was part of their power."[21] Fifty years later, at Jimmy Kimmel's suggestion, Lear revived *All in the Family* for an evening, replacing some older actors with younger ones, drawing fresh interest from a much younger generation. The influence of the TV comedy had taken hold, though Lear himself is the first to acknowledge that the problems he poked fun at have not been resolved. Still, in discussing the impact of his sitcoms on politics, Lear argued that "culture change was what demanded political change."[22]

And listen to Lin-Manual Miranda:

> What I can tell you is that works of art are the only silver bullet we have against racism and sexism and hatred. Joe Biden happened to see Hamilton on the same day James Burrows was here. James Burrows directed every episode of *Will & Grace*, and remember when Biden went on *Meet the Press* and essentially said, 'Yeah, gay people should get married'? He very openly credited *Will & Grace* with changing the temperature on how we discuss gays and lesbians in this country. It was great to see Jim Burrows and Joe Biden talk about that, and Jim thanked Biden and Biden thanked Jim because that was a piece of art changing the temperature of how we talked about a divisive issue. It sounds silly. It's a sitcom, but that doesn't make it not true. Art engenders empathy in a way that politics doesn't, and in a way that nothing else really does. Art creates change in people's hearts. But it happens slowly.[23]

Like Nathan Cummings and Unbound Philanthropy, the Ford Foundation was also drawn to the idea of using an experimental lens to learn how to intervene in the pop culture world with themes and narratives that reached a mass audience. Embracing the notion of failure and experimentation to inform their work, their interests continued the inquiries put forth by Brown and the arts for justice funders.

Building on recommendations from the *#PopJustice* report, a network of philanthropic leaders led by Unbound, Nathan Cummings, and Ford pooled resources to create the Pop Culture Collaborative, a multiyear, multimillion-dollar philanthropic fund to transform the "narrative landscape" around people of color, immigrants, refugees, Muslims, and Indigenous peoples, with an emphasis on those who are women, queer, transgender, or disabled.

The collaborative launched in summer 2017 under the leadership of chief executive officer Bridgit Antoinette Evans, professional artist and 2015 Nathan Cummings Fellow, and chief strategy officer Tracy Van Slyke, a former journalist and progressive media publisher, to drive social change through narrative development via the entertainment industry and other forms of pop culture. A new initiative was born. In their first five years, the collaborative raised more than $25 million, quickly helping to establish the still-evolving field of narrative change–based initiatives. In 2020, their funded projects cumulatively reached over 100 million people.[24] And an increasing number of foundations began to use narrative and culture shift concepts as central components in their theories of social change.

Funding Film and Culture Change

The use of films in social change goes back more than a century, starting with the very first feature-length film *The Birth of a Nation* (1915), which the KKK used to dramatically expand its membership. More recently, moving in a progressive direction, the Ford Foundation, along with MacArthur, Open Society Foundation, and other funders, began supporting independent documentaries, some going back, as is the case with Ford, to the experimental films of the 1950s.

JustFilms is among the most recent catalytic initiatives of the Ford Foundation.[25] Launched in 2010 under the leadership of Darren Walker, then vice president of Education, Creativity and Free Expression, and spearheaded by filmmaker Orlando Bagwell, JustFilms was a $50 million, five-year initiative for the creation of social issue documentaries and effective audience-engagement programs around them. This was right before the streamers Netflix, HBO, and others emerged. Bagwell's successor, Cara Mertes, the former director of the Sundance Institute Documentary Film Program, also tapped these funds to support field-building and infrastructure through which to support nonfiction films and an international network of creative documentary hubs. Mertes raised funds not only for film but for specific work in the entertainment industry and organizing community, from writers' rooms to comedy shows with an edge. Mertes said she was "investigating the question of what difference stories make, and how to expand resources beyond documentary, beyond content funding, into narrative analysis and larger integration of different fields that combine activism, organizing, impact, and creative storytelling."[26]

Recent Trailblazing

The work of the Art for Justice Fund (A4J) and the Constellations Culture Change Fund initiative reflect two of several new trend-setting practices: (1) soliciting strategic advice from those closest to the ground, or partnering with practitioners; (2) engaging in donor-to-donor organizing; (3) overcoming obstacles created when foundations silo art and organizing; and (4) putting transformative philanthropy into action. The following is the political backdrop to these two initiatives and a more detailed look at these practices.

It was the "fierce urgency of now," to quote Dr. King, that motivated A4J to spend out their assets—more than $100 million—from Aggie Gund's sale of the Lichtenstein and the additional contributions made by others, by 2023.[27] Their work reflected philanthropy at its best during the six years they were making "good trouble."

Some 2.4 million people, more than anywhere in the world, disproportionately people of color, are in U.S. prisons and jails. Another 4 million people are on parole and under supervision. The fund's immediate goal was to distribute $20 million a year for five years to disrupt the penal system, including the cash bail system that locks people up solely because they cannot afford bail.[28] Why, as Catherine Gund asked, "set up a fund that exists for one hundred years or in perpetuity when we're trying to end mass incarceration now?"[29]

At the national level, new momentum for criminal justice reform had begun to take hold in the early twenty-first century, as a consensus emerged on the left and right that something needed to be done to reform the system. In 2008, Congress passed the Second Chance Act, which provided for prisoner reentry services and programs. In 2010, President Obama passed the Fair Sentencing Act to reduce the disparities in penalties between crack and powder cocaine. In 2018, even Trump signed reform legislation, which he called the First Step Act.

Symbolic of the moment, in 2018 the Marshall Project, which curates reporting on mass incarceration, sponsored events featuring Koch Industries' vice president and general counsel Mark Holden, who outlined the archconservative Koch brothers' support for ending mass incarceration and allowing formerly incarcerated people to vote. The picture of the ACLU and the Koch brothers finding overlapping areas of interest made the possibilities for enacting legislative reform seem real. To catch the wave of bipartisan interests, a large infusion of resources to the field would be necessary.

Strategic Advice from Those Closest to the Ground

Many newer philanthropies start with the understanding that the people closest to the problems are closest to the solutions, but they are often furthest from the resources needed to tackle toxic systems. As such, A4J's funding decisions are informed by a host of stakeholders who represent voices with experiences well beyond those of their staff and board, including artist-activists, curators, and writers who were formerly incarcerated, people who lead the movement to end mass incarceration. A4J project director Helena Huang notes that "we are in relationship with movement leaders—artists and organizers—so none of our decision-making happens in an elite vacuum."[30]

By bringing together people from different sectors to inform their grantmaking decisions, A4J also built an infrastructure of activists promoting reform. As of this writing, a quarter of A4J grants, some $30 million, has gone directly to formerly incarcerated artists and organizers and the organizations they lead, as well as to children of incarcerated people and survivors of violence.

In 2019, the Kresge and Surdna Foundations engaged a design team to create the Constellations Culture Change Fund initiative, a three-year fund with the goal of raising and distributing $23 million to build an infrastructure of artists and cultural strategists to accelerate narrative changes for work on a host of issues.[31]

This fund, co-founded by artist-activist Favianna Rodriguez, was born as a collaborative effort to develop a new field of cultural strategy driven largely by BIPOC and LGBTQ activists. Grant recipients are selected by practitioners, not funders. F. Javier Torres-Campos, the director of Surdna's Thriving Cultures program, comments that they are "trying to cede power in order to seed transformation."[32]

And like the Art for Justice Fund, Constellations is resourcing individual artists. The Center for Cultural Power, an Oakland-based nonprofit that supports artists to engage in social action, manages the decentralized fund. As of late 2021, Constellations raised $10 million with a boost from MacKenzie Scott, the former wife of Amazon founder Jeff Bezos, who awarded them $8 million to support their work. Scott's philanthropy created what is now a mixed pot of funds from both individuals and institutions to support artist organizing through Constellations.

Donor-to-Donor Organizing

Donor organizing is on the rise, reaching a scale it has not achieved before. A4J project director Helena Huang said, "Donors should not be making strategic organizational decisions, nor should we be doing forced marriages" (referring to a practice among funders that provides funding for an operation contingent on specific organizations working together). Rather, she said, "We should find more ways to relieve the organizers of having to raise the money. We should use our leverage as funders to help raise money for them and go to our [funder] peers to do that."[33]

To complement their grantmaking, A4J is actively raising funds through what Huang calls a "capital aggregation model." Aggie Gund's lifelong reputation and dedication to artists, who know she values their relationships above their artwork, inspired many gifts to A4J. Two artist gifts, in particular, reflect the depth of their relationship to each other and their belief that criminal justice reform is a core civil rights issue of our time.

First, in 2019, painter Mark Bradford created an artwork entitled

Life Size, a molded paper sculpture of an LAPD body camera, to draw attention to police violence, racial bias, and surveillance. Bradford questions the purpose of the body cam to increase transparency of police conduct by creating an object that is the opposite: black, opaque, and ominous. He created a limited edition of forty-five prints and donated all the proceeds—$1 million in total—to A4J. His generosity galvanized a cascade of artists to contribute their work to the A4J fund, including Nick Cave, Jeffrey Koons, Stanley Whitney, and Titus Kaphar.

Abstract artist Julie Mehretu, who sold her painting *Dissident Score* (2019–21) for $6.5 million and donated all the proceeds to A4J, would say that, in a way, the fund has "been hundreds of years in the making."[34] Complementing artist support, galleries like Hauser and Wirth and Marian Goodman, auction houses like Christie's, and art brokers like Artsy all pitched in. In total, over and above Gund's donation, the fund has raised $25 million.

To catalyze a change on the scale of ending mass incarceration, Grantmakers will need to offset an $80 billion-a-year prison-industrial complex that includes privatized jails and related interests that are invested in its own survival. Rather than spending a small portion of money from their endowments for annual grants to organizations in the field, they are thinking about the needs of the field and are aggregating capital to fulfill them.

As a time-limited fund, in A4J's final year, instead of raising dollars to reallocate to the field, staff and board members began asking donors to contribute directly to the organizers and artists—helping funders enter into direct relationships with those doing the work. They also connect grant-seeking organizers and artists who might otherwise work in isolation from each other, in the hope of building a thriving community long after the fund has sunset. Dave Beckwith, former director of the Needmor Fund, argued that it is in the mix of these relationships that great organizing and art are produced and funding for them is made accessible.[35]

It's simple stuff. Like the Venn diagram we all learned about in classrooms, it is those overlapping concentric circles that make intersectional work possible and form the basis for organizing, whether that be donors, community organizations, or artists.

A narrow but growing sliver of philanthropy is taking Huang's admonition to heart. For instance, Torres-Campos, who is interested in building an infrastructure to support culture shift through narrative change programs, estimates he now spends 30–40 percent of his time raising money from other foundations. He says, "Our perception is that a progressive narrative change infrastructure does not exist that can rival the systems and structures that have been built by funders like the Koch brothers for generations."[36]

Many of these donor-organizing initiatives are conducted by funders who view their funds not as separate pots of money, though they may continue to fund organizations separately, but as part of a shared pot that funders can strategically deploy for greater impact when their goals and strategies for reform align.

Chloe Cockburn, a painter who started serving as a program officer with the Open Philanthropy Project Fund, a 501(c)(3) private foundation, and the Open Philanthropy Action Fund, a 501(c)(4), said she gave away some $25 million a year to "keep people out of the jails."[37] Donor organizing consumes all her time. "I think about the speed at which wealth is accumulating right now and the capacity of even one individual to dramatically change how a field is working."[38] Imagine just one donor among many from the tech or real estate sectors who pledges $1 billion to end mass incarceration. That resource alone immediately alters the funding landscape.

While some high-net worth individuals, like Gund and Dustin Moskovitz, a co-founder of Facebook who is funding Open

Philanthropy, are organizing their peers, their upfront-capital approach complements the work of more traditional social justice foundations. The more traditional foundation is set up for perpetuity and is not dependent on the whims of individual donors, who may decide to fund an issue one day then withdraw that funding the next. These foundations can play a unique long-term role in building and sustaining vital ongoing infrastructure support for the field and can provide expertise honed from years of experience on a particular issue. In many ways, this long-term strategic practice is every bit as essential as large-scale immediate funding.

Siloing Arts and Organizing

Many foundations establish internal policy goals and ask their program officers to develop grantmaking strategies to reach them. The absence of any kind of co-creation or decision-making in concert with the community can be problematic. One foundation department will fund climate policy by making grants for science, advocacy, and civic engagement, while another department will fund racial justice. Art and culture departments fund art programs and capital projects. But rarely are their strategies entwined, even when they focus their grantmaking in the same issue areas.

Bullitt Foundation executive director Denis Hayes notes,

> There's a whole lot of siloing going on . . . the staff that is working on the environment doesn't talk to those working on social justice, who don't talk to those working on education who don't talk to the staff working on the arts.[39]

This forces a grant seeker to choose between submitting proposals

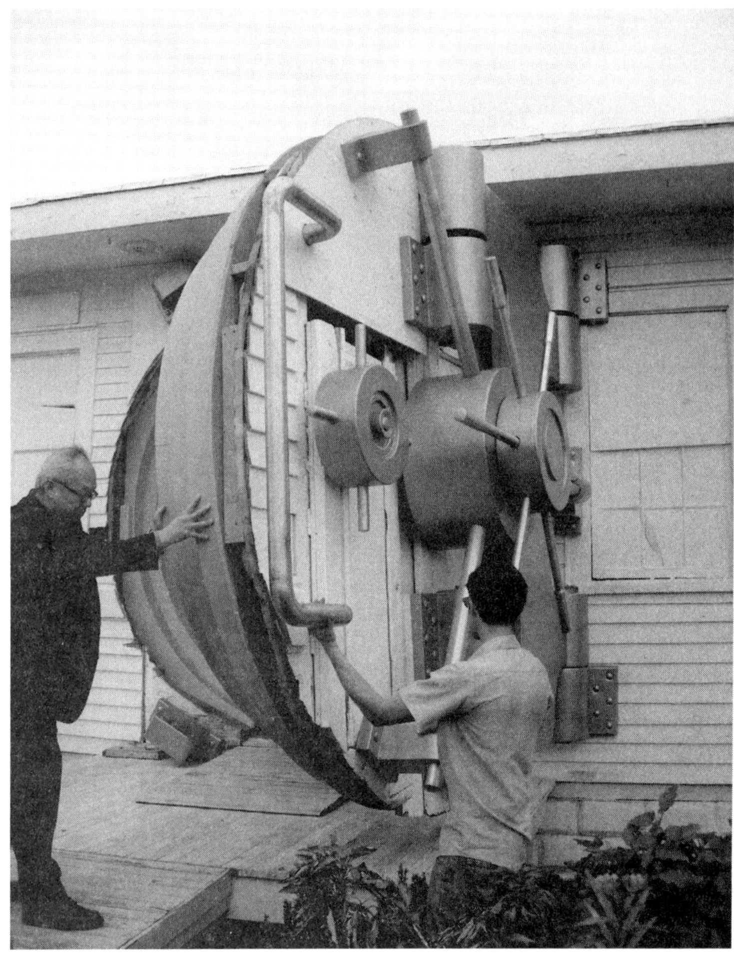

Conceptual artist Mel Chin opening the bank vault door he installed on the facade of a home in the 8th Ward of New Orleans. Photo courtesy of Micheline Klagsbrun, 2009.

for conventional community organizing and voter engagement and engaging artists to create artwork that will give expression to social justice but may exclude organizing.

For instance, conceptual artist Mel Chin's Fundred Dollar Bill Project (2008–21) was a thirteen-year-long national initiative to combat childhood lead poisoning, spanning science, art, and organizing.[40] In the aftermath of Hurricane Katrina, Chin focused on soil analysis in New Orleans that proved lead contamination and calculated the amount of money it would cost to remediate the contamination.

Through schools and community institutions, the project organized kids (and their parents) to create and donate individual "fundreds," a personalized version of a single hundred-dollar bill, as a symbolic contribution to end the threat of lead. Chin transformed a house in the 8th Ward into a bank, cutting a ten-foot circle through the facade to create a bank vault door leading to a bank where the fundreds were deposited and community meetings held. The spectacle of the vault filled with fundreds highlighted the crisis.

Chin then went one step further. He used a decked-out armored truck to pick up and carry the contributions from city to city, collecting fundreds at schools and community centers across the country. Each stop drew more national attention to the issue and generated momentum for activists and community organizations working to protect children from exposure to lead and other toxic chemicals in the soil. Reflecting on the Fundred project, Chin said,

> We've created a format for kids who could not vote, who are being poisoned, to draw their own hundred-dollar bill. It started with one hundred right there in the 8th Ward of New Orleans, and it moved all over the country to get a half million. . . . My greatest joy is when a child from some city would draw a fundred, knowing that their voice had agency and importance against this problem.[41]

Chin's work exemplifies the way science, art, and organizing can be indivisible in this type of project. Yet some practitioners feel pressed to compartmentalize their work and redefine their goals to accommodate funder interests. They ask themselves if they should pitch their work as an organizing, arts, or science project.

When funding is awarded to reach large-scale goals, such as ending racism or mass incarceration, all types of organizing campaigns, artwork, and narrative shift initiatives may contribute toward reaching the goal. That's how the real world works. But when foundations isolate funding for art and culture programs from funding for organizing and policy, they may fragment and diminish the impact of their financial support, because this approach to grantmaking may not strategically consider the various forces in play. The work of the Art for Justice and Constellations Funds avoids these pitfalls exactly because their work is informed by practitioners.

Transformative Philanthropy in Action

A4J, like several other funders, developed numerous strategies to end mass incarceration, from straightforward civic engagement focused on electoral work to the socially engaged practices of artists and museums, writers and publishers, performers, directors, playwrights, and theaters.

One of the many collaborations between emerging artists and high-profile institutions A4J supported featured the work of portraiture artist James "Yaya" Hough, who was imprisoned for twenty-seven years. Hough became the first artist-in-residence in the Philadelphia District Attorney's Office, where he created engaging portraits of formerly incarcerated people, public officials, prosecutors, and judges. *See Plate 6.* The portraits hang in district attorney Larry Krasner's lobby, a stark contrast to the black-and-white mug shots the public is accustomed to seeing on "Most Wanted" flyers. Krasner comments, "I think that it's important we never dehumanize any of these folks. And art does that. Art works against dehumanization."[42]

Hough's growing body of work was recently featured in an exhibition at MoMA PS1 and entitled *Marking Time: Art in the Age of Mass Incarceration*, curated by Nicole Fleetwood. He is now working along with A4J to set up similar art residencies in district attorneys' and public defenders' offices throughout the nation. These unusual collaborations alter how the public views criminal justice. They certainly humanize the situation.

One among many high-profile civil engagement initiatives A4J supported was Florida ballot initiative Amendment 4, to restore voting rights to former felons. Here's the story:

In 2018, the Florida Rights Restoration Coalition (FRRC), led by Desmond Meade, an author, lawyer, and civil rights activist and organizer who was formerly incarcerated, forged an alliance with the Brennan Center for Justice, a law and policy institute, and Faith in Action, a community organization that focuses on mass incarceration, to draft a ballot initiative to amend the state constitution. The proposed constitutional amendment would allow felons who served their time, including parole or probation, to vote by eliminating the requirement to pay fines, fees, and restitution.[43]

Most returning citizens can't afford these costs, which all too often run into the thousands of dollars. Some restitution orders are more outlandish, such as the $190,000 the court ordered Coral Nichols to pay stemming from a grand theft conviction, or the $59 million the court ordered Karen Leicht to pay for restitution for federal insurance fraud.[44] These costs are clearly prohibitive and result in Florida's modern-day poll tax disenfranchising roughly 1.4 million voting-age adults. A Republican-dominated state legislature and Governor Ron DeSantis sought to protect their incumbency by regulating the composition of the electorate. The restoration of voting rights required an act of the Governor's Clemency Board.

The FRRC led a movement of formerly incarcerated people, their families, and allied community organizations collected eight hundred thousand signatures to put the ballot initiative up for a vote. Emblematic of a social change campaign that embraced artists, donors, community organizations, and legal advocates, Meade and the FRRC's efforts focused both on shifting state policy through the ballot and on shifting narratives that paint formerly incarcerated people as unworthy to participate in our democracy.

Lifting up the personal stories of formerly incarcerated people adversely affected by the inability to restore their citizenship rights, Meade references a firefighter in Putnam County, Florida, who was convicted of a felony for a bar room fight. He was seeking to have his rights restored so he could go on school trips with his daughter. Countless stories like this surface regularly among those who are often invisible to the general population but whose votes conservatives fear.

The multipronged field operations included one thousand formerly incarcerated people and their families from twenty-five states who helped knock on doors. (Those who were not able to canvass reached residents by text and phonebank.) That act itself broke the public stigma associated with returning citizens right at the doorsteps of these communities. It humanized the methodical process of collecting petition signatures and the rigors of turning out the vote. In discussing the impact of the canvass, Meade notes that it was a "50/50 proposition," by which he meant that canvassers hoped to dispel myths and turn out the vote, but the residents on whose doors they knocked also altered the canvassers' perceptions of reality.[45] It was a two-way street that laid the groundwork for follow-up. It also boosted turnout among low-propensity voters.

Performing artists played an outsized role in raising funds and engaging audiences statewide. Among the most notable was singer-songwriter John Legend, who invests heavily in racial justice and has a profound command of the issues and strategies for reform. In 2014/15, Legend organized a listening tour to learn more about criminal justice issues and the organizations advocating for reform. Inspired by the work of activists like Meade, Legend immersed himself in the Amendment 4 campaign. His tweets, public statements, press events, and performances spread the word to millions of his followers. For a moment, pop culture took center stage. In the Maynard Evans High School auditorium, he performed Bob Marley's "Redemption Song," along with his own musical hits. He rallied the Orlando community and went door to door to turn out the vote.

Legend was not alone. Lady Gaga, Ariana Grande, and rapper Vic Mensa all urged their audiences to sign the petition for voting rights at their respective concerts. Mensa went one step further and offered to autograph pictures of himself with his fans if they signed the petition. When artists harness their celebrity and communicate with their fans, whether through concerts or through social media, they can reach millions. The buzz they generate also reduces voter engagement campaign costs, as the campaign would have had to find an alternative means to reach voters statewide.

Red-and-blue tour buses, painted by artists, went city to city from the east coast of Florida to the west, north, and south of the state and to the Florida Keys, featuring the images of formerly incarcerated people and the sign "Let My People Vote, Vote *Yes* on Amendment 4." Public buses carried a variation that declared "When a debt is paid, it's paid." *Let My People Vote* (2018) was also the name of Gilda Brasch's award-winning short documentary jolting through Florida and elsewhere. English and Spanish language ads permeated conventional and social media. T-shirts were emblazoned with another message: "Past mistakes should not define a person's future."

The Art for Justice Fund was one of many funders, including Open Philanthropy and the Marguerite Casey Foundation, that provided money to the FRRC and the campaign, followed by a significant and varied group of donors from corporate and labor supporters to legal advocates and others. To win, Huang said it took an estimated $20 million in c4 money, on top of the c3 foundation support.[46]

Nearly 65 percent of Floridians voted to pass Amendment 4. It is a prime example of an initiative driven from the bottom up, supported by institutional philanthropy and individual and corporate donors, that successfully challenged state power by unraveling racist narratives and forging a broad alliance of organizations that delivered a decisive victory.

Unwilling to concede, in 2019 DeSantis signed SB 7066 to disenfranchise at least 774,000 former felons by reinstituting a version of the poll tax.[47] The fight continues.

Transforming Philanthropy

Cultural philanthropy has come a long way since the early part of the twentieth century when it mostly funded elite art institutions and excluded communities of color. In a break from the past, a larger collection of philanthropies are asking community allies to inform their funding decisions rather than relying just on their staff and boards for input. Dana Bourland, the senior vice president for Environment and Strategic Initiatives of the JPB Foundation, said their "investments in climate justice organizations [for instance] are driven partially by movement organizations telling them that the arts are a critical component of what is needed to help tell the story."[48] Grantmaking through the Constellations Fund is made by practitioners. A4J relies heavily on formerly incarcerated people and their allies to inform their funding choices. Most recently, the Mellon Foundation committed $125 million for art projects to counter the effects of mass incarceration.

This vital work is beginning to transform how some institutional and individual donors operate. The overlapping relationships among funders, artists, and community allies are key to successful organizing and narrative shift programs. They form an essential and necessary infrastructure through which change can be won.

When cultural philanthropy collaborates with the communities it wants to serve and gives up some power and control, it often strengthens its work. By adopting a crucially important and necessary equity imperative, these funders can grapple with their troublesome past and respond more effectively to movements for social and economic justice.

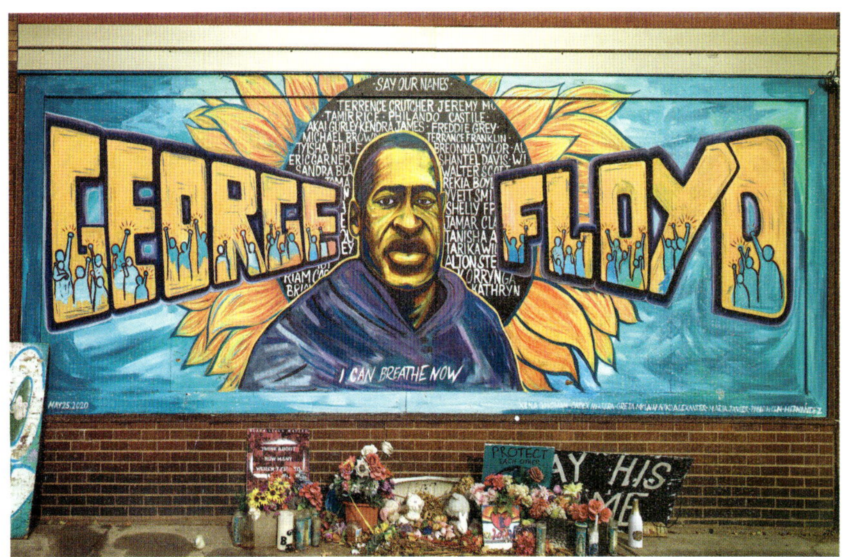

Plate 1. The first of hundreds of murals honoring George Floyd and calling for justice, by Xena Goldman, Cadex Herrera, and Greta McLain, Minneapolis, 2020. Photo courtesy of Carol Highsmith/Library of Congress.

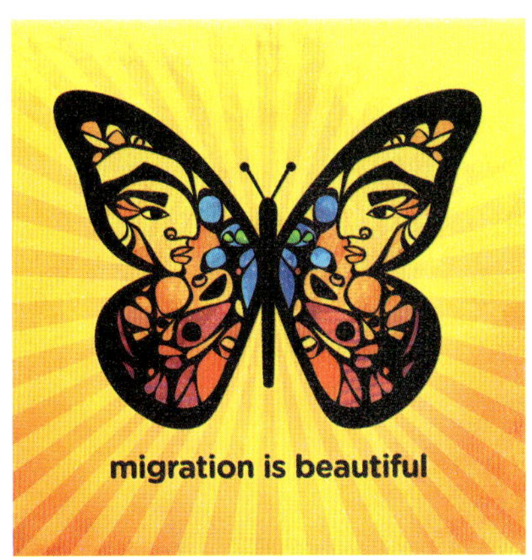

Plate 2. Migration Is Beautiful, *by and courtesy of Favianna Rodriguez, 2018.*

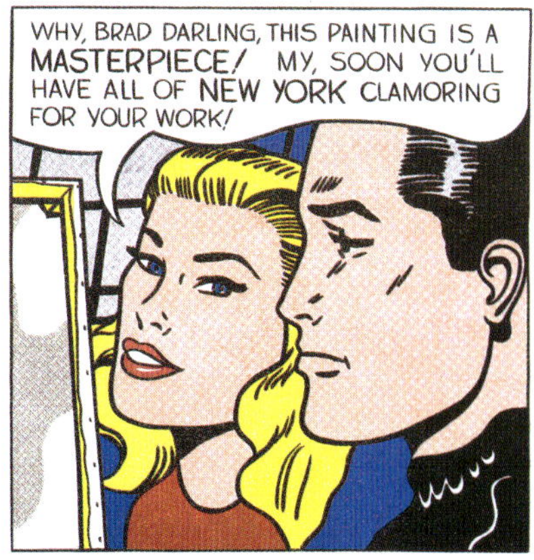

Plate 3. Masterpiece, *by Roy Lichtenstein, 1962, © The Estate of Roy Lichtenstein.*

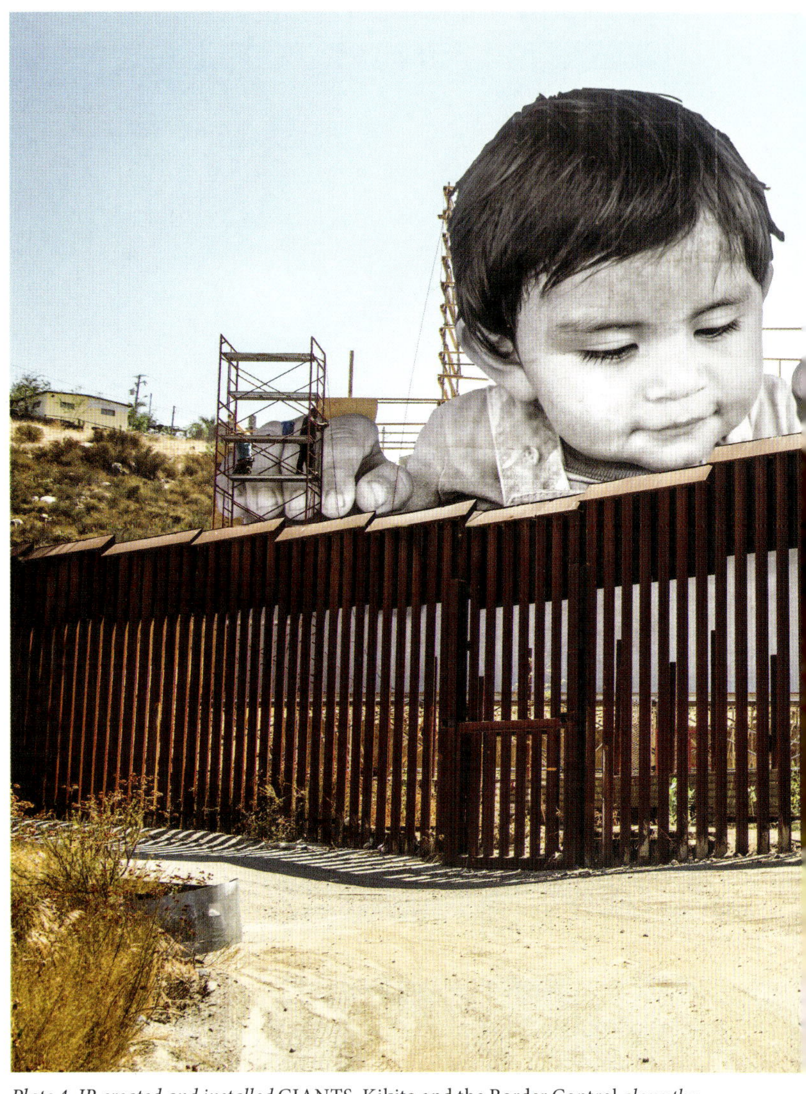

Plate 4. JR created and installed GIANTS, Kikito and the Border Control *along the U.S.-Mexico border, 2017. Mural and photo © JR.*

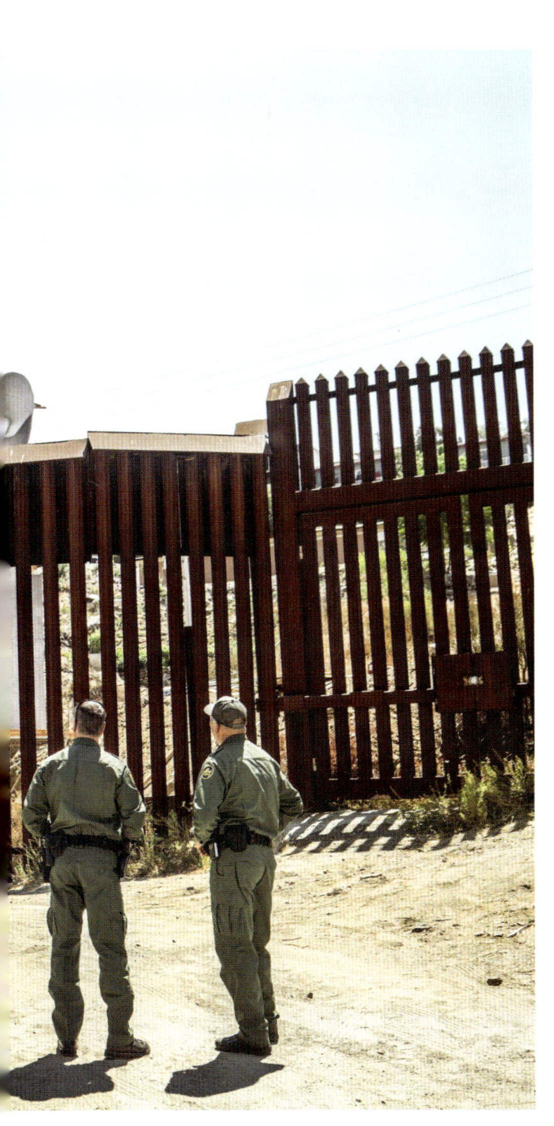

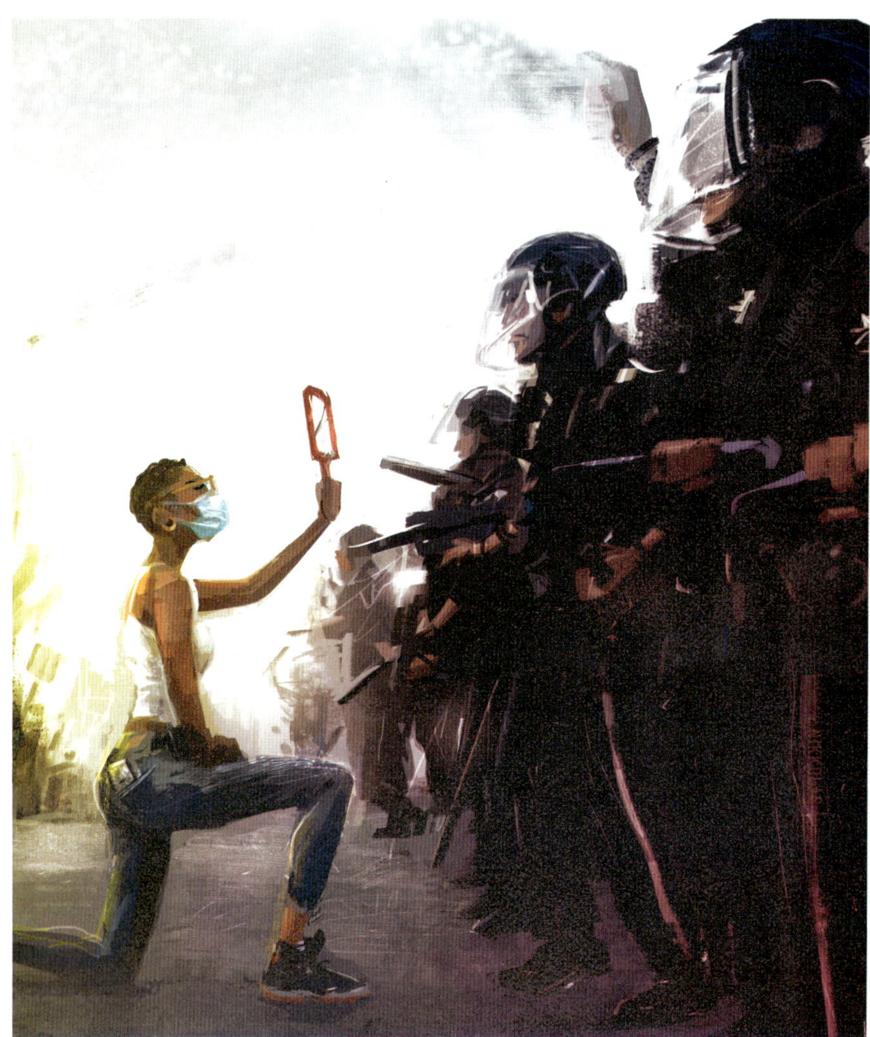

Plate 5. Reflect, *by Nikkolas Smith, © Nikkolas Smith, 2020.*

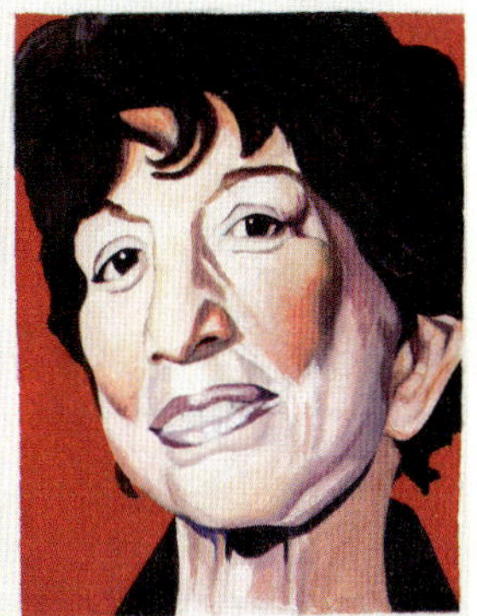
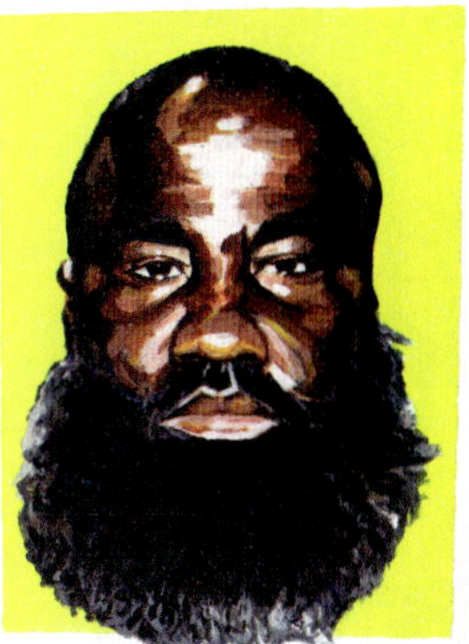

Plate 6. Portraits by James "Yaya" Hough, the first formerly incarcerated artist-in-residence at the Philadelphia District Attorney's office, 2020. Photos by Akeil Robertson/Mural Arts Philadelphia.

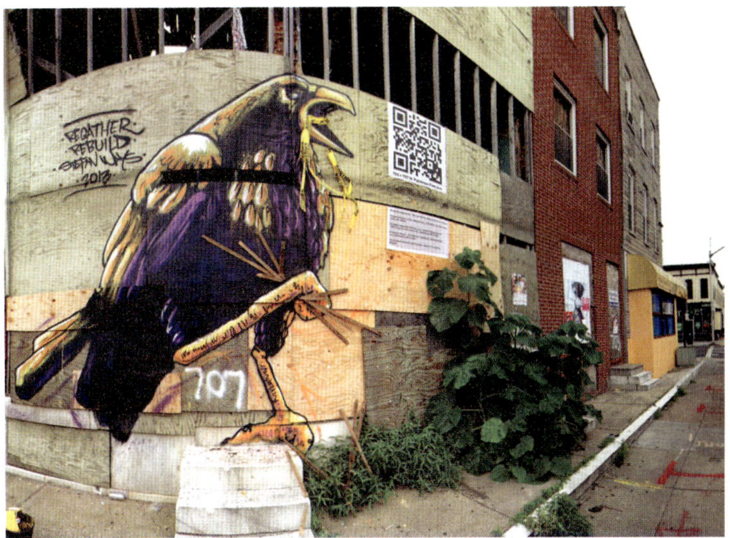

Plate 7. Raven, *by Stefan Ways, Baltimore Maryland, 2013. Photo courtesy of Justin Nethercut, 2013.*

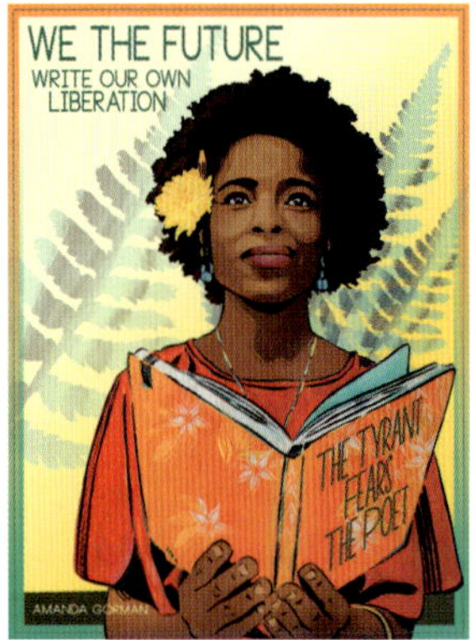

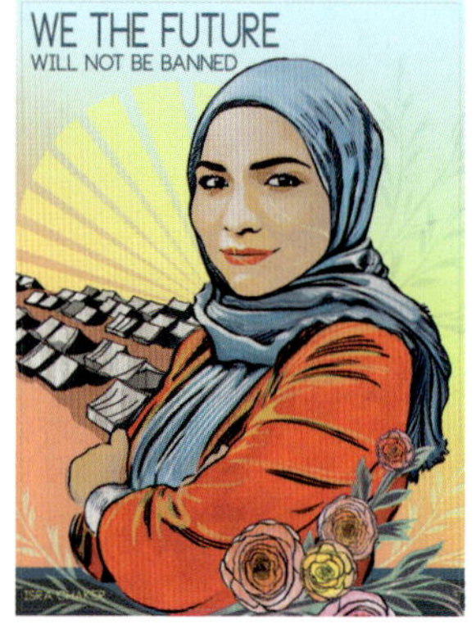

Kate Deciccio

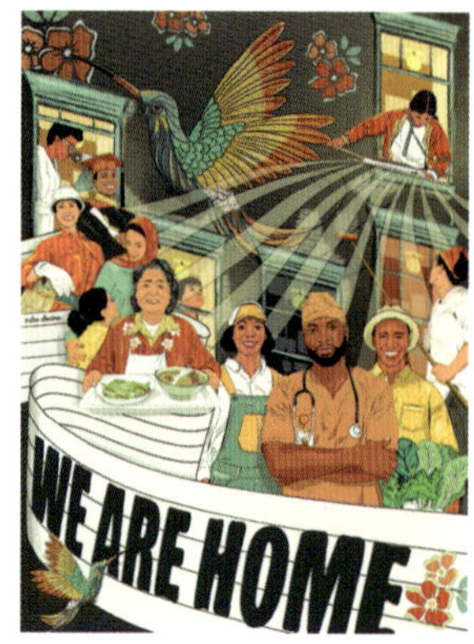

Alex Albadree

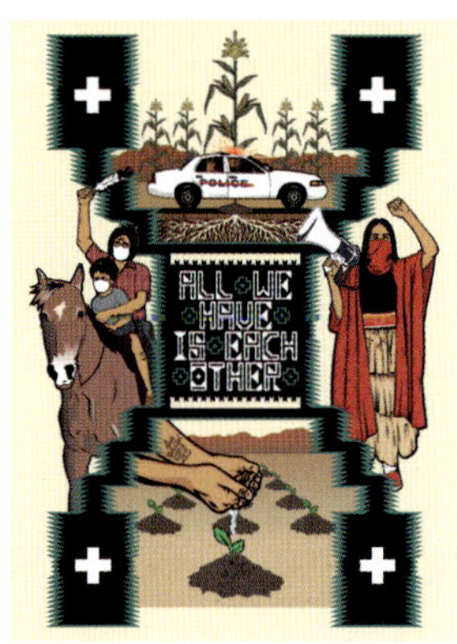

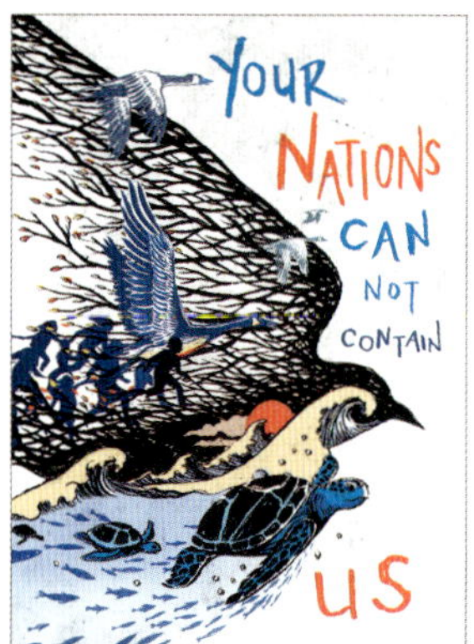

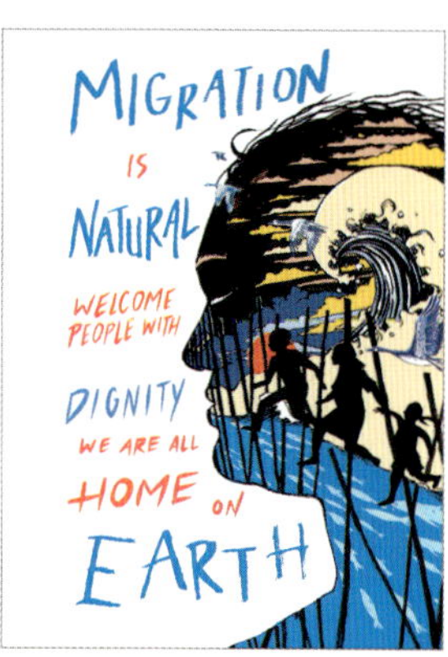

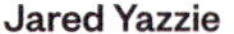

Jared Yazzie

Jess X Snow

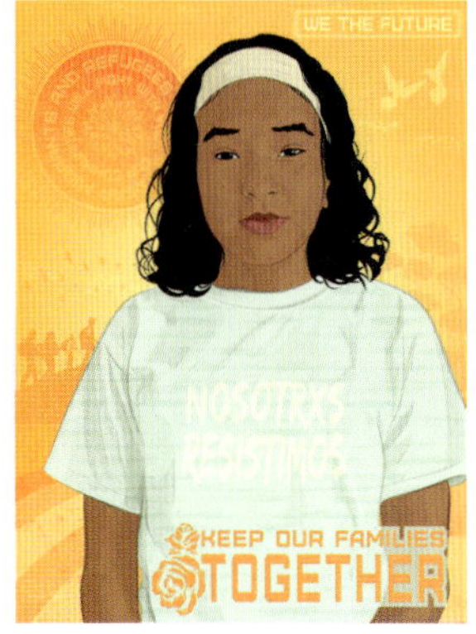

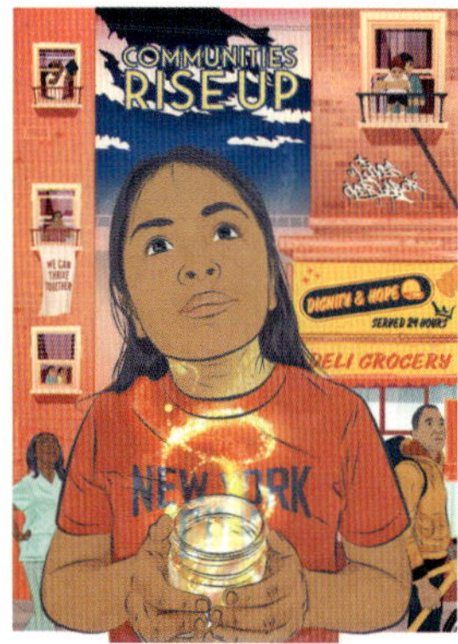

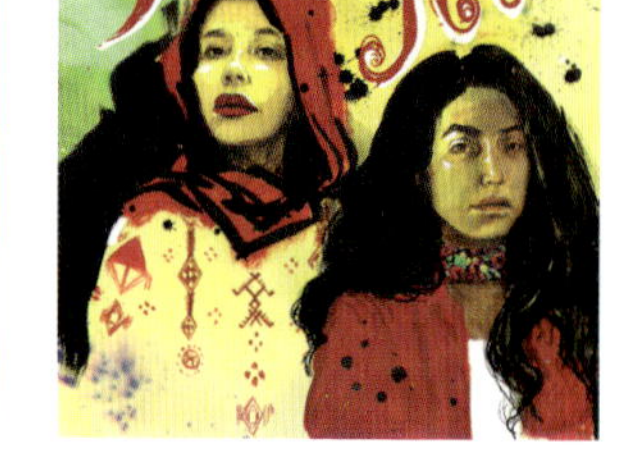

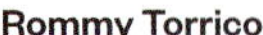

Rommy Torrico

Molly Crabapple

Plate 8. Poster art display by Amplifier, 2020. See page vi for individual poster credits.

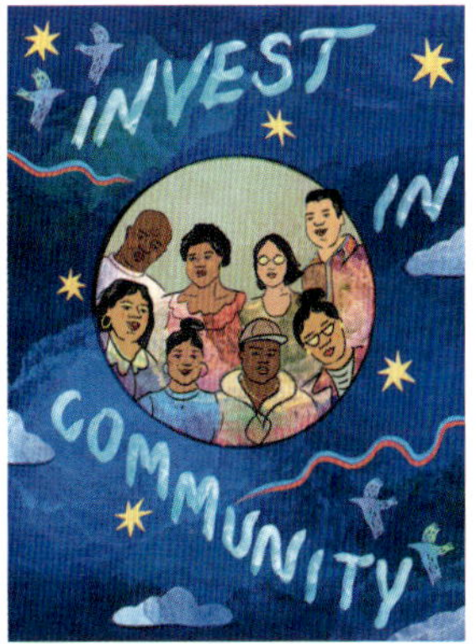

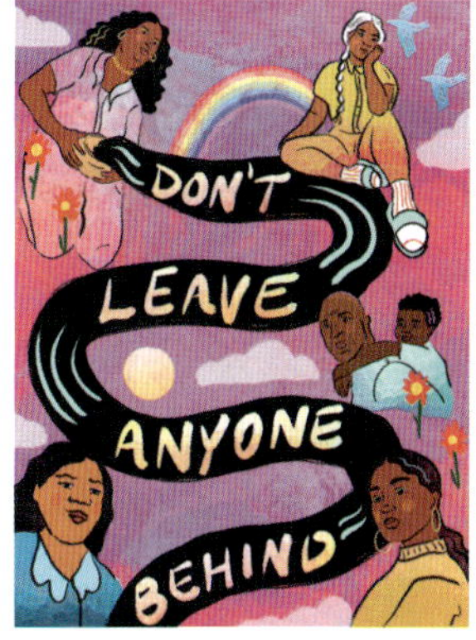

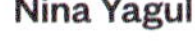
Nina Yagul

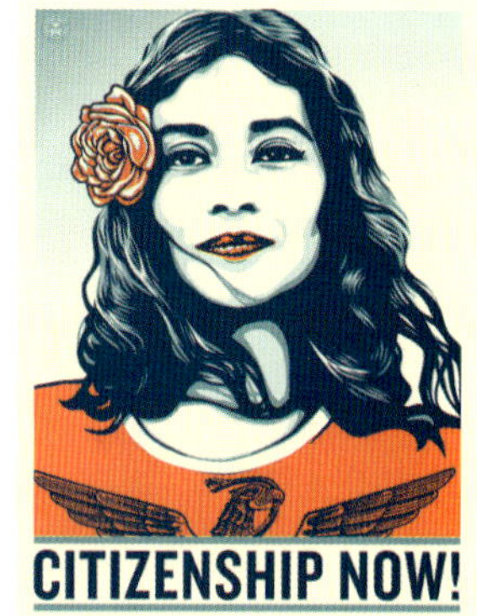

Shepard Fairey

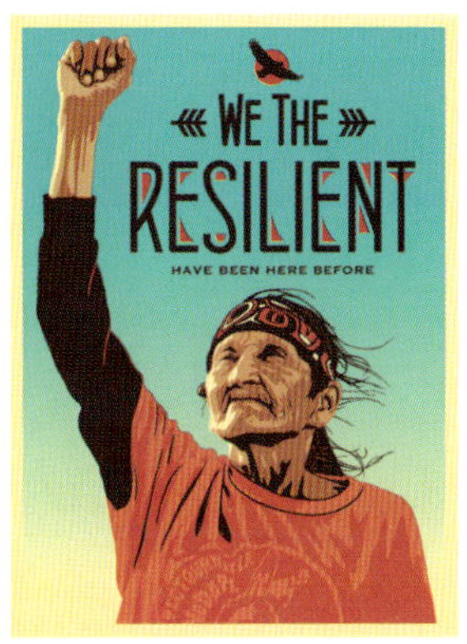

Ernesto Yerena

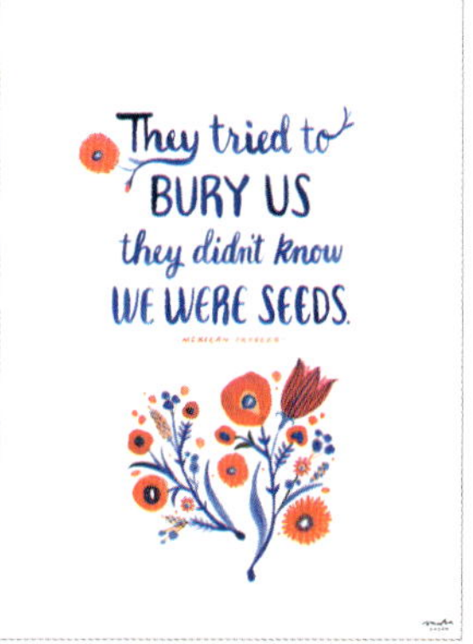

Misha Zadeh

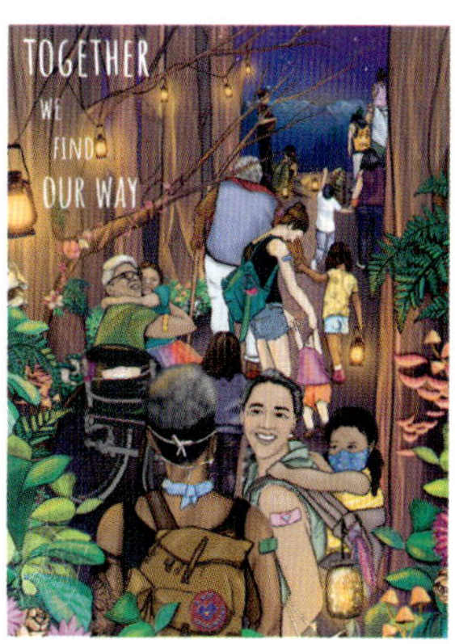

Rue Oliver

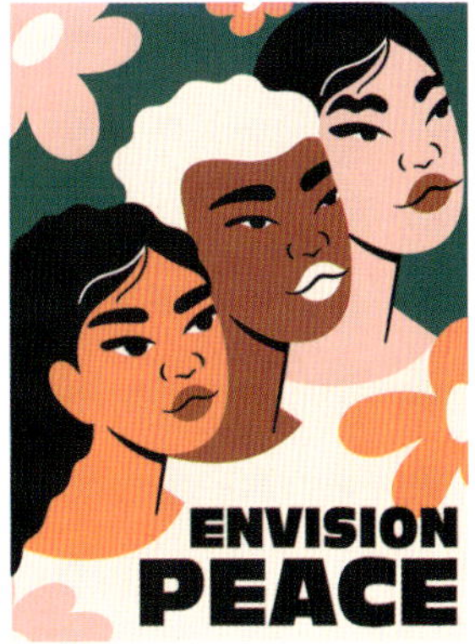

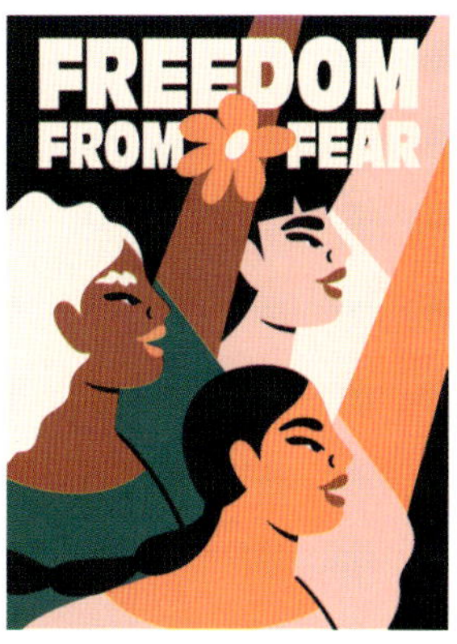

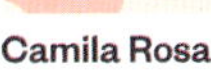
Camila Rosa

Unapologetic Street Series

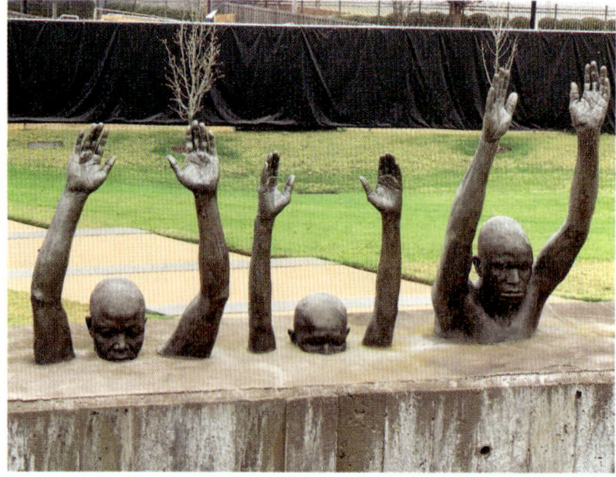

Plate 9. Raise Up, *a partial view of Hank Willis Thomas's sculpture at the National Memorial for Peace and Justice, 2014. Photo courtesy of Micheline Klagsbrun.*

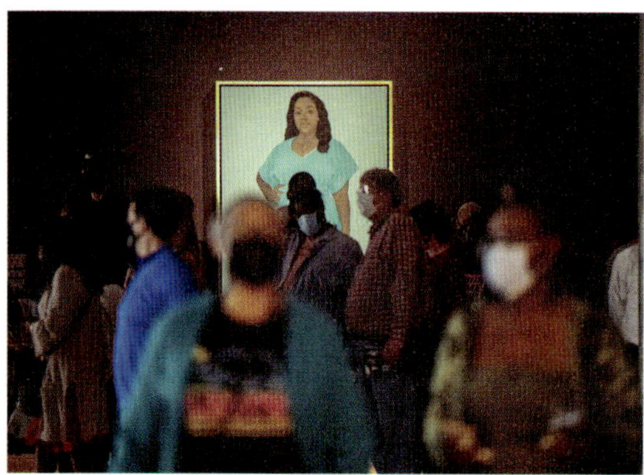

Plate 10. Amy Sherald's portrait of Breonna Taylor became a centerpiece of the Promise, Witness, Remembrance *exhibition, Speed Museum, Louisville, Kentucky, 2021. Photo courtesy of Jon Cherry, 2021.*

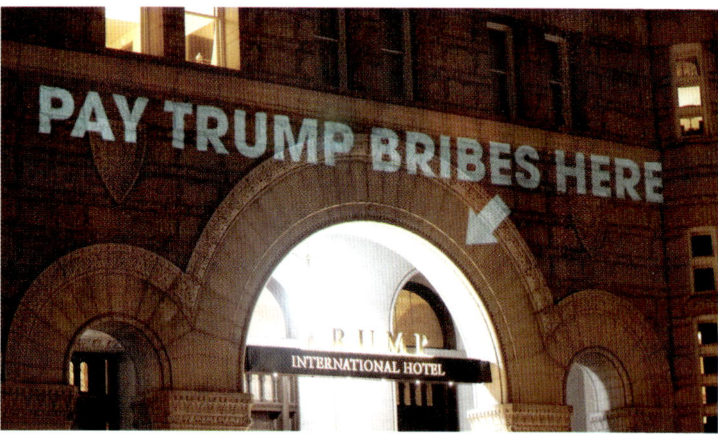

Plate 11. Robin Bell's Pay Bribes Here, *a digital projection Bell cast on the Trump Hotel, 2017. Projection by Robin Bell. Photo by Liz Gorman.*

7

Afterword

Artists and Organizers Speak

The stories of organizer and artist-activist collaborations across art genres propel the preceding book chapters. This chapter is propelled by their ideas.

In June 2022, I had the privilege of hosting a roundtable discussion with a diverse and intergenerational group of prominent strategists from within the artist-activist and organizing communities. My goal was to capture their voices on some of the many issues reflected in the previous chapters. We discussed basic but perennial issues, including the relationship between art and social change, the value of and obstacles to collaboration among artist-activists and organizers—what works and what doesn't—and the impact of commercial industries and culture that define and sometimes dominate our historical views and current frames of reference.

The roundtable was facilitated by artist Michael Premo, the founder of Storyline, and included long-seasoned leaders in their fields: artist-activist Shepard Fairey, conceptual artist Mel Chin, longtime SEIU labor organizer Josie Mooney; rapper Jasiri X; Sonya Childress, co-founder of Color Congress; artist-organizer Aisha Shillingford; and community organizer George Goehl. What follows are excerpts from our conversation, edited for brevity and clarity. The sections in italic are written by the author.

We are in a moment when community and labor organizers, artists, and narrative change advocates are searching for movement-building approaches to develop more powerful alliances to tackle persistent issues of our time. Over the last two decades, they have begun to merge and synthesize their ideas and practice, and many of these strategists are experimenting with new forms of collaboration in their respective approaches to social action. What do you think is the relationship between art and social justice, and how does it inform your theory of change?

Sonya Childress: A Perspective from the Documentary Film Community

Films really animate our radical imaginations.[1] They help us visualize new possibilities. When the light comes up after a film is screened, there's that catalytic moment where people are having an emotional response to a film. And in that moment, there's an opportunity, sometimes a very small opportunity, to shift assumptions, shift thinking, shift behaviors, shift relationships, shift resources, and ultimately shift power or challenge it. And you must anticipate that catalytic moment and have a way to move people from that emotional response to art into some kind of action. Impact producers are essentially tasked with conceptualizing a strategy for how this one piece of media, one piece of art can reach its highest potential as a tool for change.

Many filmmakers of color do not think about change goals in terms of shifting legislation or policy or getting people out into the streets. They see their films as for their own communities, as a tool to confront and heal wounds that we can't engage in organizing. We can't step into advocacy positions until we address some of the personal traumas that are holding solidarity and agency back.

Jasiri X: Art Rooted in Community

Coming into the world as a Black man, automatically, my existence becomes political just when I take my first breath.[2] So, I come into a world and witness injustice and want to change it. And for me, I was born at a time when a genre of music called hip-hop came and gave a voice to people that look just like me.

I feel like the movement work came first, and out of that work comes my music, organizing, and how we create change in our community. My art and music are connected to the work that I do every day. It has the most power when it is rooted in movements. When creating art is rooted in community, it becomes art for social change.

Josie Mooney: A Level of Engagement the Labor Movement Didn't Have

Art brings an important level of engagement that we [in the labor movement] have not always had.[3]

Saul Alinsky said that all organizing is the art of developing relationships, and the way you get authentic relationships is to ask questions. We ask people to tell their story and connect their story with the next person's story. We weave together people's culture, experience, and lifelong lessons. We try to come up with a strategy that unites. When I was growing up, the big art would be a sign that says "On Strike," period, or "Unions Now," period. There would be no cultural engagement. There would be no different language engagement. There would just be "strike."

We need to deepen our engagement with artists so that we can be more effective organizers. Art illuminates culture and can help transform how people participate in collective action.

Shepard Fairey: Creating Space for a Different Narrative

[Originally] I recognized the power of art in culture, not through visual art for the most part, but through music, through punk rock, reggae, and hip-hop.[4] And whether it was the Clash, the Dead Kennedys, Bob Marley, Public Enemy, people who were using their art form to talk about social issues in a way that had a visceral enjoyment, it had its own culture on its own terms. It's creating space for a different narrative than the dominant narrative. I wanted to speak to a broader audience than the usual elitist art institutions, galleries, museums, academia, and connect with people.

I looked at a lot of the cultural vehicles that you find in entertainment culture, but especially music culture, where there's an accessibility, there's building a connection with a group of people who are like-minded, and then seeing the ripple effects that happen and taking it directly to people instead of having them come to you. As an artist I was going to use the street. I also started to pair early on with people [and organizations like] the Sierra Club and with marginalized communities reentering society after incarceration. I didn't have a grand plan, but I just knew this was the kind of stuff that seemed like a more meaningful use of my talent. And then I stumbled through figuring it out and I'm still figuring it out.

The value of collaboration seems self-evident; it's a way to pair political action, messaging, art, and culture shift work to build power and solidarity. Yet, for some organizers and artists, collaboration can be a diversion and it is not without its difficulties. In part, that is because the historical culture of social change organizations has not fully embraced the arts as a strategy to move their agenda forward. Similarly, many artists opt not to collaborate or deploy their work in the service of social movements. What are your views on the value of collaboration?

Sonya Childress: Alchemy Through Art

There's an alchemy that gets catalyzed with a piece of art. You [can] brain trust it with a diverse set of stakeholders by bringing together journalists, organizers, educators, policy makers, folks from philanthropy, and different sectors, [who] look at the project before it's reached an audience and to talk about what unique role it can play, say in [the] educational space, as an organizing tool, or as a healing tool.

In some ways that meeting [engages] people who don't usually see themselves as artists, who don't usually engage in cultural organizing, but they have an opportunity now to collaborate with one another, for some co-creation, for some trust building, for some collaboration among people who may not actually see themselves as allied because the social justice ecosystem is so siloed—with some people working on immigration, some in criminal justice, and other issues.

I have found that coming together around a table and a particular piece of art allows for some of the silos to come down for a moment. And then for all of us to imagine the ways that our separate movements, approaches, strategy goals, and strategic communications can be subsided for some collective action. Art allows people who don't usually engage with art as a tool to develop really different kinds of relationships together, which ultimately supports more than just the vision of a particular artist, but movement building.

Jasiri X: Collaboration Has to Be Organic

I'm for collaboration. In some ways, as Black people, we're always looking for that Black united front. I remember early in my career as a hip-hop artist, Professor Griff came to me and he said, "You know, Jasiri, I love what you do, but you're by yourself," which is something that always resonated with me, that I didn't want to be the sole person on the stage. I learned collaboration has to be organic. If it's forced, it always turns out terrible. If we can collaborate, and it could be done in a way where everybody feels validated, everybody feels like they have the agency, I'm for it.

Mel Chin: It's Part of the Job Description

[For artist-activists,] collaboration is part of the job description.[5] And we owe it to our partners, whoever we work with, to be engaged in self-critical dialogue about what we are precisely doing.

> *Yet historically, many community and labor organizations have not opened themselves to new forms of collaboration. They're at a crossroads in thinking through strategies that merge organizing with culture or narrative change work. What guides your thinking about integrating art and social justice organizing?*

George Goehl: We Bring Not Bread, but Yeast

I was raised as an organizer to not include art in our work.[6] We certainly weren't encouraged to do it and probably discouraged. But that never really made sense. There's so much at the core that's deeply aligned. I've always loved James Baldwin's words that "artists are here to disturb the peace," which is, I think, exactly what organizers think of as their job. Organizers are agitators. We bring not bread, but yeast. Our job is to agitate people, to ask hard questions and see things in themselves that they wouldn't see until we came into their lives.

There's a lot of common ground that we share, but we don't always recognize and make those connections. Artists are often able to move big ideas into the conversation well before the country, place, or people are ready. In many ways they are an advance team, [offering] a critique of what is, and a vision that reaches people untouched by organizing. I think organizing does this too. We have a unique role in turning what people now call narrative change into tangible change in people's lives. Our job is to take advantage of this opening, whether that's in policy or practice. Teaming up is a powerful place where we can do more together.

Josie Mooney: As Labor Organizers, We Have a Lot to Learn

We weren't trained to think about art. Those of us who have been labor organizers a long time were trained to singularly knock on doors to secure the vote. There was no engagement. We were trained to make an assessment and move on. We were not trained to learn a story, connect the story, encourage, and be encouraged through the exchange. So I think we have a lot to learn.

Shepard Fairey: Collaboration Is Essential to Building Movements

I think that collaboration isn't essential in all forms of art, but in building movements it is because you need the power in numbers. I mean the forces of oppression have economic leverage, mercenaries willing to work for them. And they're all going to collaborate whether we're looking at it in the way we're defining it or not. And so to push back against that and create a better path, you have to have movements that are built on collaboration and power in numbers.

When I look at all the things that I'm taking into consideration as a visual artist, trying to have a social message and the problem solving of how aesthetics are going to lure the person in or provoke the person to think about something they wouldn't think about otherwise, how to then work with other people to get on the same page. It's especially valuable when you hear what other people think, and weave that into your own strategy while they then learn something from you.

It's not always easy. So, I look at all of this stuff as kind of it can't all be pleasurable. Part of it is work and it's work I mostly take joy in, but if you really believe in just living day to day in a way that is going to help to shape the world into one you'd rather live in, then it's just part of it. You just accept that. And every night you need the right rhythm.

It should go without saying that mutual respect is a prerequisite for successful collaborations, but it requires an understanding of the interests of each party and defining the terms for the collaboration. How do you approach collaboration?

Shepard Fairey: "I Have to Feel Proud of My Work"

I'm very receptive to people coming to me, but what I explain to them is ultimately I have to feel proud of the work I'm doing. So, this is going to be an exchange. And if we get to a point where you feel like what I'm providing is not delivering on what you want or I feel like what you're asking for, I can't be proud of, then let's just be respectful and go our separate ways. Now that almost never happens, which is a beautiful thing. But I think it's very helpful to put that idea out there so that people don't get as touchy and don't get their feelings hurt as easily because there is a lot of subjectivity in how this stuff works. I like to be a good listener, but I have strong opinions.

Michael Premo: Not an Advertising Agent

Things are changing, but there have been instances when I've collaborated with folks on a storytelling project, and they just treat me like I'm some kind of advertising agency.[7] And sometimes maybe that's all that's needed for a project, and that's fine, but not treating an artist as a real strategic partner is a missed opportunity. And if you are committed to transformational change, then why treat artists in such a transactional way? There will be a tendency to micromanage every detail of what is being created. And I have to go, "Look folks, I love you. But how much do you love me?" If you value the strategic leadership of community members, why not extend the same to the community members who are artists? Thankfully, this is starting to change, but we have a long way to go.

George Goehl: There's Some Stuff We Have to Get Better At

When we reach out to artists after the strategy is baked, the plan is developed, and the action is designed, it is too far down the road [for the collaboration to succeed]. On the other hand, such as in cinema, when a film is done and it's coming out in five weeks, and then we get a call to organize around the project, it's not like we're twiddling our thumbs thinking we wish we had an idea or something to do.

Aisha Shillingford: Not Aestheticizing Protest

[Organizers sometimes] narrow the role of artists to what we will call aestheticizing protest.[8] I was trained in the Alinsky school, [and in my practice] we decided twenty years of organizing is enough to trust ourselves, to translate what we understand the vision and values of movement to be. We dream to be in relationship, where we establish political alignment with what the groups are doing on the ground, the evolving visions of communities.

Though many artist-activists play key roles in social movements, some are marginalized, not given seats at the strategy table, and their work is not readily accepted unless it checks off the many boxes organizers and communication strategists need checked. Others find that dominant commercial interests in culture don't support, or worse, intentionally exclude their art from mass exposure. How do you think about this?

Jasiri X: Socially Conscious Music Connects

People told me nobody wanted to hear socially conscious music. When I put "Free the Jenna 6" song out, it played across the country, and it becomes like a theme song to a movement. It showed me I can create something and use my voice to connect with these larger movements for change. What I've sometimes experienced is when a person brings me in, they then almost become afraid of what I create. Then they start to think about funders and older folks, and then what I create gets cut down.

I did a song around Trayvon [Martin], and I remember it was the first time I wanted a call to action connected to a video, because at this time George Zimmerman [who killed Trayvon Martin] hadn't been arrested. I contacted Rashad Robinson [president, Color of Change], to me, one of the most amazing organizers of our time. I wanted kind of a Color of Change piece. I sent him the video and the song, and he was like, "I don't know about this line or this line." I was like, "Hey, Rashad, this it, bro. Are you rocking with me or not?" And this is my man, Rashad is my buddy. We put it out and it connected.[9]

So I would say now, if you want to engage me, it's either all or nothing. It's either you're going to allow me to express myself, or just let me be in Pittsburgh, doing my thing.

Aisha Shillingford: "I Need Some Autonomy"

If you came to me because you like my art, I need some autonomy in deciding what it is. We need to understand the terms of collaboration and agree on them.

> *Working across diverse communities challenges activists to be sensitive and defer to different community needs, desires, and ideas. Seasoned organizers and advocates know that to succeed in building alliances, the interests of community organizations are paramount. Yet artists are frequently confronted by communities that are skeptical that their intervention will matter and critical of extractive practices that promote the artist and work of art but does nothing to build community. What has been your experience?*

Shepard Fairey: A Contested Mural in Milwaukee

In the 2020 election, I had been invited to paint a mural in Milwaukee, and I wanted to do an entire group of murals in battleground states, collaborating with the ACLU, but that ended up being derailed by COVID. But I still had the opportunity to do one mural in Milwaukee. The mural I was going to do was a mural that said, "Voting rights are human rights," that was a collaboration with civil rights photographer Steve Schapiro. He had 1965 images of the Selma to Montgomery civil rights march, and one of a Black activist marching for voting rights, with the word "VOTE" written on his forehead.

And I wanted to say, "Hey look, fifty years has passed, plus, and we're facing all the same threats to voting rights, voter suppression, democracy itself now. And I've been invited by the building owner to do whatever I wanted, and this is what I wanted to do." But some of the local activists said, "You're making a mural about issues that deal with people of color, you shouldn't do it as a white person." And some people just tried to block it altogether. The plan was also to make a print of the mural and donate the money to a couple of local voter registration organizations that were mostly directed towards communities of color, which I thought was very important. I was frustrated because I tried to be an ally, but I understood why they were frustrated, because so many great nonwhite artists are passed over for opportunities. But this wasn't something that was put forth by a city-funded organization, this was just a private building owner.

So, I took a deep breath and said, "Some of the mean stuff that's being said about me is really wounding and hurtful. I just want things to move in a better direction and voting Trump out is going to be essential to that. That's a step." But then I just decided, all right, let me reach out to community members who are artists and see about what collaborators I can bring in representing a lot of the different groups. I had a Zoom and said, "Look, I'm sorry if I didn't reach out to the right people in advance, my intentions were good, maybe my tactics were not as smart, but let's have a discussion about this. I want to hear from all of you, what you think. This is a mural that if I don't do it, it's not going to happen, but I have the opportunity to bring collaborators in and make it be bigger than something just about me."

I said, "I've gotten a lot of opportunities that probably came to me just because I'm white. I'm going to listen to people vent about opportunities that they feel they haven't gotten because they're not white and see where we can find common ground on how to approach this mural, to move forward together." It ended up being a beautiful project. The Milwaukee Bucks got behind it and promoted it. The voting organizations were happy about the money they got. It required a lot of putting ego aside and just talking through things.

And what I have to say is that for all the times I felt my throat tighten up and I felt like I was being punished for trying to do something that I felt was pushing things in the right direction and I was trying to be a good ally, I understood the pain and frustration. And I just said, "Let's get past that, and let's find some common ground and move forward." And that's what we did, and I'm proud of it in the end.

Mel Chin: Turning Plastic Bottles into Swimwear

Art takes many forms, such as my Flint Fit Project around drinking water in Flint, Michigan. I got Tracy Reese, a fashion designer who created the dress Michelle Obama wore at the 2012 Democratic National Convention—where President Obama was nominated. I got a company in North Carolina which changes plastic bottles into fabric, and a sewing center, the New Life Sewing Center in Flint. The idea was to convert plastic into swimwear. I had a presentation for the people of Flint. It was important to get permission. So, I called the activists that were in Flint that were fighting for clean drinking water. I wanted to hear them first. They said, "All right, so you're an artist. So, what the fuck you going to do for us? Obama's been here,

Hillary's been here, Trump's been here, and maybe even Brad Pitt, and we still don't have any clean drinking water. So, what could you possibly do to help get us there?"

I told them I'd explain the project, and if you say, "Get out of here," I walk. The idea was for them to collect bottles and we would put them in a truck and take them down to North Carolina and turn them into fabric, and Tracy would create swimwear ideas, and then we'd sew them up in the sewing center and create a fashion line. They said, "Okay, we got it. We want you to do it." We did. I'm so proud that Tracy moved from NYC to Detroit, and that she is still working with that sewing center, which supports women who have experienced domestic abuse and trains them how to sew. At first, she didn't believe they could do fashion, but she's still working. I'm still here and they're still sewing clothes.

Strategic communication is a critical element of all social movements. We've suffered from bad messaging and benefited when it reflects public opinion and our base. What are some of the difficulties we have to navigate between communication strategists and artists?

Aisha Shillingford: Sometimes We Speak Different Languages

I noticed that often organizations aren't sure if they're wanting a graphic designer or an artist.

Josie Mooney: The Language of Art Can Be Different Than Communications

I would say to an artist on our staff, we always want there to be a clear message. He said, "Yes, but if you let me be more creative, the message could be stronger than you telling me to say something like 'staff up

San Francisco.'" He advised we were being too formulaic. I've learned when organizers collaborate with artists our work is more powerful.

Shepard Fairey: Facts Don't Matter Unless We Are Emotionally Primed

I think that messaging is always important, but sometimes when I'm working with people, they're approaching things in a way that puts the intellectual communication ahead of the emotional impact. And there've been study after study that show that people don't really care about facts unless they're emotionally primed to care. And so you got to lead with something that's emotionally resonant.

And that's the beauty of good art, is it also takes people out of a zone where they're just going to follow their default disposition on an issue, and maybe there's that space for evolution that comes with emotional intrigue. And so I've found over and over that if I just made the images that I think will, you could say seduce, lure, Trojan horse the challenging idea that people need to evolve on, into the art, and then I'm developing kind of an arsenal of those things.

Perennially, commercial industry interests are at odds with movement goals, and yet provide a platform for artists and organizers to reach a mass audience with their message. How do we grapple with their dominant interests in a way that exploits the resources they bring to bear while not being co-opted?

Shepard Fairey: Co-opting Culture and Not Being Co-opted

I'd like to chime in a bit about art versus commerce, the co-option of culture, because I see this all the time. I have my own clothing brand, I've been doing art for musicians, art in the streets. I've seen a dramatic evolution from being considered a vandal, to now being considered a gentrifier. I'm wrestling with these things all the time, but I do think that it's important to look at the fact that commerce is one of the languages that people speak. It's part of culture. It has many, many downsides, capitalism. It's a brutal system. But also, if you try to avoid it, you're really existing in isolation without any potency. I look at it like, there's the concept of detournement, using the machinery against itself, infiltrating the machinery, making it think that you're its friend, and then planting a seed that gets people to question the nature of that machinery itself, or you could say in martial arts, using your opponent's own weight against them.

This is part of the creative collaboration when your collaborator is somebody that doesn't think like you. You're infiltrating, and you have an opportunity to change things for the better from within the system or sit it out and let them co-opt what you do in a degraded, safe, counterproductive way. I choose to try to navigate all this stuff with idealism and realism merged, and be a pragmatist, and not about, okay, these are good-paying jobs, I just got a good check from Netflix, but how am I going to write the contract so that I have creative control and I get to use their very big megaphone to help me?

And I know this is always very difficult stuff, but sometimes, I feel frustrated about the defeatism I hear when culture is being co-opted and people are acting like they have to just stand there as spectators and watch it happen, and they can't actually be part of the process of making that move in the most ideal direction possible, rather than just being angry about it.

Mel Chin: How Can We Make History?

One of the most interesting projects of collaboration was something we did as a covert entity called the GALA Committee, made up of students, artists, critics, producers, and set decorators. We worked with commercial television as a site for education. We made sure that some of our collaborators were the actual producers who became part of the team. We inserted artwork [two hundred pieces] on a prime time soap opera called *Melrose Place* for two years. We made props and made adjustments—top secret. We inserted messages—broadcast to millions. And it was important [both] to look at it and not to look at it as a subversive situation, but to say, "How can I reach a producer and make history with them?"[10]

Michael Premo: Using the Commercial Platforms

Documentaries have never really been commodified at the scale they are now, but suddenly, the commercial TV and film industry is discovering their commercial potential. But that doesn't have to be a bad thing. There's a long history of artists who can use that [commercial] platform to do really provocative things

Sonya Childress: Can We Protect the Art?

The documentary industry's being overwhelmed by commercial platforms that have a very different mandate than public media, that was really about ideas. The commercial mandate is about profit, and yet these commercial streamers are co-opting, I would say, the language of social justice, are reaching out to documentary filmmakers of color for the first time in the last two years. They are saying, "Make a film about an organizer. Make a film about the undocumented organizing effort. Make a film about the labor movement. We'll give you money you've never seen before as a documentary artist. We'll give you a huge budget to make a film about something you really care about as a socially engaged filmmaker, and your stuff is going to be seen by millions, the biggest audience you might ever reach." And people are hearing the language, they're hearing the words, they're seeing the opportunity.

Organizers are like, "Yes, we'll bring you our stories, we'll be subjects and we'll be participants in those films, we'll be on camera." Filmmakers and narrative change folks are finding this moment exciting, and yet these streamers are also wielding huge editorial control over these stories. They are pushing these films into singular-hero narratives, character-driven, take this analysis out, make it broad, make it sexy, make it sensational, go into a community, and take the story out, and do it in a way that's extractive so it can turn a bigger profit. All of this stuff is really distorting the artistic practice, distorting the values that the project is supposedly under, while using and co-opting that language. It's hurting movements and the practice of artists. Commercial interests are always going to be one step ahead, with something shiny which could disrupt and undermine.

Aisha Shillingford: Making Work That Reveals the Truth

How do we build the power of artists inside of culture industries? And how do artists organize to shift industries that they're in, sometimes not by choice.

We've been thinking in my studio [Intelligent Mischief] about the roles of artists that are making work that reveals the truth, artists that are working to shape values and vision, and the future that we're moving toward, artists that are creating relief for communities that might be facing oppression and injustice and designing spaces that are the areas of reprieve. How do we expand and see artists interacting with all aspects of change, thinking of artists as strategists?

Sonya Childress: Building Off the Power of Culture

What's great about this moment is that it is building off the power of culture. It's starting there. There's a unique and important role that culture plays in social justice organizing, and a special role that artists play within the social justice ecosystem. The embedding of artists within movements is a durable approach to social change.

The stories of seasoned and accomplished activists, like those in the roundtable, illustrate how successful collaborations among artist-activists and organizers have helped to achieve social justice. Each chapter serves not as a strict prescription for change, but a strategic guidepost for impact.

Organizers are shifting how we do our work. Community and some labor organizations are opening themselves up to new forms of collaboration with artist-activists, who in turn are developing a field of "cultural organizing." Meanwhile, new collectives and organizations of artists are burrowing into and sometimes leading the long-term work of building movements.

Even mainstream institutions are getting into the act. Large foundations committed to equality are investing more heavily in marginalized communities working for change, and in art that supports social justice. Museums are slowly but increasingly moving toward developing community alliances that focus on people first, objects and buildings second.

History will judge the impact of these shifts in practice. But the promise of these collaborations renews the possibilities for creating lasting change. Art Works *offers practical models designed to propel their promise into the future.*

ACKNOWLEDGMENTS

Many leading lights in movement politics helped me to think about and frame the ideas in this book. They put up with my writing insecurities, offering critiques, suggestions, and guidance, chapter after chapter, that immeasurably strengthened my work.

Dave Beckwith, an organizer's organizer, died in 2022, but his ideas about how to change the world remain alive and course through each chapter. I endlessly sought advice from Denise Mitchell, the most effective communication strategist I know, who offered it with grace, clarity, and punch. Drawing on forty years of experience as a musician, playwright, author, and organizer, Si Kahn, in what seemed like weekly conversations, offered a steady stream of insights that breathed life into my work.

I owe a debt of thanks to several friends and colleagues who read and commented on specific book chapters. Ron Simon was my toughest critic. Pat Aufderheide, Lou Cohen, Bill Fletcher, Jill Hartz, Taryn Higashi, Helena Huang, Jennifer Lawson, Suzanne Little, Cara Mertes, Diana Schemo, and Pamela Yates all contributed ideas that made a difference.

To close the book, I hosted a diverse and intergenerational exchange among strategists in the arts and organizing community doing the work this book describes. Many thanks to Wendy Levy, who helped organize the roundtable discussion, and to each strategist who participated, including Sonya Childress, Mel Chin, Shepard

Fairey, George Goehl, Jasiri X, Josie Mooney, Michael Premo, and Aisha Shillingford. This book celebrates their voices and practices.

Thank you to the New Press team, including Diane Wachtell, who took a risk with a sixty-eight-year-old guy who had never written a book, and for the strong editorial support of Nikki Moran and Marc Favreau. Thanks also to Athena Angelos, who procured many of the images in the book.

There are two people without whom this book would not have been written. In the 1980s, my mentor, scholar-activist Richard Cloward, helped shape my political ideas and orientation to politics and social movements. He taught me how to think strategically and encouraged me and his many students to express and act on dissident ideas. Though he may not have agreed with all that I posit here, I hope my book lives up to his radically influential expectations.

My wife, DC-based artist Micheline Klagsbrun, inspired me to write this book. In concert, we delved into the relationship between art and politics, bringing together my background in community and labor organizing and her knowledge of art history and experience making art. It wasn't until we each figured out the other's language that this book project launched. In addition to reading every draft, while simultaneously converting my writing into English, she's been my partner each step of the way. Her love sustains me.

INTERVIEWS

More than a hundred organizational leaders, prominent artists, academics, and community and labor organizers graciously informed my work on this book. Prior to the pandemic, we talked in person, and subsequently, through Zoom interviews. I'm indebted to them for the work they do and their ideas that grounded so much of my thinking.

Ai Weiwei, Elizabeth Alexander, Pablo Alvarado, Christian Arte-ga, Bill Ayers, David Bacon, Barbara Schaffer Bacon, Dave Beckwith, Gina Belafonte, Dana Bourland, Jackson Browne, Sarah Browning, Margaret Caplez, Jeff Chang, Caty Borum Chatoo, Sonya Childress, Chloe Cockburn, Michelle Coffey, Dianna Cohen, Julia Cohen, Courtland Cox, Peter Coyote, Damon Davis, Paco de Onís, Kirby Dick, Bernadine Dohrn, Geralyn Dreyfous, Beka Economopolous, Eve Ensler, Bridgit Antoinette Evans, Tom Finkelpearl, Jane Fonda, Ellen Friedman, Michael John Garces, Miki Garcia, Todd Gitlin, Danny Goldberg, Catherine Gund, Thomas Allen Harris, Jill Hartz, Liz Havstad, Denis Hayes, Fei Hernandez, Melissa Ho, Helena Huang, Tabitha Jackson, Jasiri X, Alan Jenkins, Cleve Jones, JR, Si Kahn, Gene Karpinsky, Maurine Knighton, Pam Korza, Dorothy Kosin-ski, Jennifer Lawson, Norman Lear, Annie Leonard, Suzanne Little, Danny Lyon, Yo-Yo Ma, Josh MacPhee, Cesar Maxit, Bill McKibben, Susan Meiselas, Desmond Meade, Paola Mendoza, Cara Mertes, Kristina Mevs-Apgar, Jim Miller, Maurice Mitchell, Sean Doyle

Morales, Molly Murphy, Naomi Nataly, Stanley Nelson, Justin Nethercut, Karen Nussbaum, Jeff Orlowski, Carol Ott, Erin Potts, Gordon Quinn, Stephen Reily , Yosimar Reyes, Joel Reynolds, Sadiqa Reynolds, Favianna Rodriguez, Maida Rosenstein, Martha Rosler, Julio Salgado, Jess Search, Yosi Sergant, EJ Serrano, Amy Sherald, Aisha Shillingford, Nina Simon, Martha Slaughter, Antonique Smith, Regina Smith, David Solnit, Jim Stearns, Noel Paul Stookey, Dan Strickland, Hank Willis Thomas, Eddie Torres, F. Javier Torres-Campos, Jose Antonio Vargas, Norm Van Vector, Steve Weissman, Rïse Wilson, Peter Yarrow, Pamela Yates, Rev. Yearwood.

NOTES

1: "Freedom Is a Constant Struggle"

1. The origin of this expression—which has slightly different versions—is thought to be drawn from the 1978 work of Greek poet Dinos Christianopoulos. More recently, it has been attributed to Mexican activists in 2013. Amanda Gordon further popularized the expression in her 2018 TED Talk entitled "Using Your Voice Is a Political Choice." www.ted.com/talks/amanda_gorman_using_your_voice_is_a_political_choice/transcript.

2. *Martin Luther King Jr. Encyclopedia*, "Songs and the Civil Rights Movement," Stanford University, Martin Luther King Jr. Research and Education Institute.

3. Mark O'Brien and Craig Little, *Reimagining America: The Arts of Social Change* (Gabriola Island, BC: New Society, 1990).

4. Danny Lyon, *Memories of the Southern Civil Rights Movement* (Santa Fe, NM: Twin Palms, 2010), 98.

5. Andrew Glass, "Civil Rights March Ends as 'Bloody Sunday,' March 7, 1965," *Politico*, March 7, 2018.

6. Author interview with Courtland Cox, October 29, 2020.

7. Susan King, "Academy to Honor Harry Belafonte for His Activism," *Los Angeles Times*, November 6, 2014.

8. Author interview with Gina Belafonte, November 12, 2020.

9. Harry Belafonte, *My Song: A Memoir of Art, Race and Defiance* (New York: Vintage), 347.

10. See Harry Belafonte, SNCC Digital Gateway, snccdigital.org/people/harry-belafonte/, and *Martin Luther King Jr. Encyclopedia*, s.v. "Belafonte Harold George Jr.," Stanford University, Martin Luther King, Jr. Research and Education Institute.

11. Tom Shales, "The Bright Appeal of Red Buttons," *Washington Post*, July 14, 2006.

12. "If it hadn't been for music . . ." is from civil rights leader and congressman John Lewis's speech at the 17th Annual Choral Tribute to Dr. Martin Luther King Jr., January 9, 2005, at the John F. Kennedy Center for the Performing Arts, choralarts.org/johnlewis.

13. For full lyrics see "Nina Simone's 'Mississippi Goddam,'" by Eli Michaud, Black Arts Movement, blackartsmovementumf.wordpress.com/nina-simones-mississippi-goddam/.

14. Written by Abe Meeropol, published in 1937, and performed initially at Café Society by Billy Holiday in 1939, billieholiday.com/signaturesong/strange-fruit.

15. Aida Amoaka, "Strange Fruit: The Most Shocking Song of All Time?" BBC's Culture: Songs that Made History, April 17, 2019.

16. Brian Pietsch, "Behind Strange Fruit, Billy Holiday's Anti-Lynching Anthem," *New York Times*, April 25, 2021.

17. Bernice Johnson Reagon, "In Our Hands: Thoughts on Black Music," in *Hands on the Freedom Plow, Personal Accounts of Women in SNCC, Sing Out Magazine* (January 1976).

18. Nat Hentoff, "What Bob Dylan Wanted at 23," *New Yorker*, October 24, 1964.

19. For more on "Keep Your Eyes on the Prize," see "Music of the Movement, Eyes on the Prize," by Jacqueline Trescott, *Washington Post*, August 24, 2011.

20. Bruce Hartford, "The Power of Freedom Songs," www.crmvet.org/info/fsongs.htm.

21. SNCC Digital Gateway, a collaboration between the SNCC Legacy Project, Duke University Libraries, and the Center for Documentary Studies at Duke University, is an ongoing website dedicated to SNCC history, https://sncCdigital.org.

22. Author correspondence with Jennifer Lawson, March 2022.

23. Jennifer Lawson.

24. Bradley George and Grant Blankenship, "The Girls of Leesburg Stockade," GPB News, NPR, August 14, 2020.

25. Danny Lyon provides a firsthand account in *Memories*, page 80. See also www.walb.com/story/5190050/stolen-girls-remember-1963-in-leesburg.

26. Matt Herron, "Proposal for a Documentary Program in Photography," SNCC Digital Gateway, a website dedicated to SNCC's history.

27. Herron, "Proposal."

28. Bob Adelman and Charles Johnson, *Mine Eyes Have Seen: Bearing Witness to the Struggle for Civil Rights* (New York: Time, 2007).

29. For a fuller discussion of this argument, see "A Conversation with John O'Neal," Junebug Productions, November 2012.

30. Andrew Salinas, "Free Southern Theater," 64 Parishes, February 11, 2016, 64parishes.org/entry/free-southern-theater.

31. Kennedy Center Education, August 10, 2017, www.youtube.com /watch?v=D0AMyilwIfo.

32. *Pins and Needles* started out in a community theater, and as its popularity rose, it moved to Broadway. AFL president William Green, Secretary of Labor Frances Perkins, and others attended the show.

33. An overview from *Pins and Needles* by director Rachel Grunwald, rachelgrunwald.com/shows/pins-and-needles.

34. Randy Ontiveros, *In the Spirit of a New People, the Cultural Politics of the Chicano Movement* (New York: New York University Press, 2014).

35. For a comprehensive overview of Teatro's performances, see "Celebrating 55 Years of Teatro Chicano," eltreatorcampesino.com.

36. Randy Ontiveros, *In the Spirit of a New People: The Cultural Politics of the Chicano Community* (New York: New York University Press, 2014), 134.

37. Ontiveros, *Spirit of a New People*, 134 .

38. Zoom discussion hosted by the Philadelphia Art Museum with poet Nikki Giovanni, 2021.

39. Poetry Foundation, "An Introduction to the Black Arts Movement," www .poetryfoundation.org/collections/148936/an-introduction-to-the-black-arts -movement.

40. "Black Lives Matter: How It Started and What It Stands For," DCP Entertainment, April 19, 2020.

41. Alicia Garza, *The Purpose of Power: How We Come Together When We Fall Apart* (London: One World, 2020).

42. Akiba Solomon, "Get on the Bus: Inside the Black Life Matters 'Freedom Ride' to Ferguson," ColorLines, September 5, 2014. See also blacklivesmatter .com/herstory.

43. Daniel Kreps, "Tom Morello Drops Protest Song 'Marching on Ferguson,'" *Rolling Stone*, October 13, 2014.

44. In a galvanizing moment President Obama sang "Amazing Grace" at the Mother Emmanuel church service held to remember those killed.

45. To watch the video "Cry No More," go to www.npr.org/2015/07/15/422949419/first-watch-rhiannon-giddens-stunning-charleston-response.

46. Author interview with Bill Ayers, November 18, 2020.

47. Dru Berry, "Artists Paint George Floyd Mural at Cup Foods," *MPLS/St. Paul*, May 29, 2020.

48. For a more comprehensive overview of these street murals, see "33 Powerful Black Lives Matter Murals," *The Verge*, July 5, 2020.

49. The Fine Acts Collective, *Rolling Stone*, and *Vice*, offer details of these posters and more.

50. Author interview with Nora Halpern, Americans for the Arts, 2020.

51. Childish Gambino, "This Is America," www.youtube.com/watch?v=VYOjWnS4cMY.

52. For example, see Staceyann Chin, "Racism," www.youtube.com/watch?v=7CKO_OETlMY.

53. To see the Dave Chappelle performance on YouTube, go to www.youtube.com/watch?v=3tR6mKcBbT4.

54. The Lee statue was removed from the public square in 2021.

55. Charles Blow, "The Great Erasure," *New York Times*, May 22, 2022.

56. Nick Cumming-Bruce, "UN Panel Takes Aim at Heavy Handed Police Tactics at Protests" *New York Times*, July 29, 2020.

57. For an overview of historic sites, including monuments and statues, I relied on James W. Loewen, *Lies Across America: What Our Historic Sites Get Wrong* (New York: The New Press, 2019).

58. Claire Selvin and Tessa Solomon, "Toppled and Removed Monuments: A Continuing Guide to Statues and the Black Lives Matter Protests," *ARTnews*, June 11, 2020.

59. Quinnipiac Poll, June 2020, thehill.com/homenews/news/503226-poll-majority-supports-removing-confederate-statues-from-public-places.

60. Virginia Museum of Fine Arts website.

61. "Kehinde Wiley: A New Republic," edited by Eugenie Tsai, in 2015, Brooklyn Museum, in association with DelMonico Books.

2: "Singing for Our Lives"

1. Northern Dynasty Minerals Ltd investment highlights, January 2008.

2. Elwood Brehmer, "Permit Application Reveals Size of Scaled-Down Pebble Project," *Alaska Journal of Commerce*, January 10, 2018, www.alaskajournal.com/2018-01-10/permit-application-reveals-size-scaled-down-pebble-project.

3. Tyler Thompson, "A Breakdown of the Bristol Bay Census Results for 2020," KDLG Public Radio for Alaska's Bristol Bay, September 24, 2021, www.kdlg.org/community/2021-09-24/a-breakdown-of-the-bristol-bay-census-results-for-2020.

4. Alaska Department of Environmental Conservation, Office of the Commissioner, dec.alaska.gov/commish/tribal.

5. "About Bristol Bay," United States Environmental Protection Agency, www.epa.gov/bristolbay/about-bristol-bay.

6. Reuters, "Alaska's Pebble Mine Told to Offset Damage as Republican Opposition Grows," August 24, 2020.

7. EPA, "2022 Proposed Determination for Pebble Deposit Area," May 2022, www.epa.gov/bristolbay/2022-proposed-determination-pebble-deposit-area.

8. EPA, "Bristol Bay," September 9, 2021.

9. Alex DeMarben, "An Epic Forecast for Bristol Bay Salmon Has Industry Leaders Worried it Will Be Too Much to Handle," *Anchorage Daily News*, April 8, 2022.

10. U.S. Geological Survey, Science Features, "The 1964 Great Alaska Earthquake and Tsunami," February 24, 2014.

11. "The Pebble Mine Promise in Bristol Bay," a minority staff report prepared for the Democratic members of the Committee on Science, Space, and Technology, April 2016.

12. Song lyrics used with permission, @JoeHill Music LLC (ASCAP), administered by Reel Muzik Werks, LLC.

13. Ilana Kaplan, "Watch Keb' Mo' Decry Single-Use Plastics in 'Don't Throw It Away' Video," *Rolling Stone*, June 16, 2019.

14. Author interview with Si Kahn, March 2022.

15. Pete Seeger video as seen on the Musicians United for Bristol Bay, www.musiciansunited.info.

16. The race's exact starting and stopping points depend on snowfall and, more recently, the COVID-19 pandemic.

17. Author interview with Jim Stearns, June 1, 2021.

18. Jim Stearns, June 1, 2021.

19. Drew Griffin, Scott Bronstein, and John D. Sutter, "EPA Head Met with a Mining CEO—and Then Pushed Forward a Controversial Mining Project," CNN, October 24, 2017.

20. Brandi Carlile, Facebook page, August 4, 2013.

21. Jim Stearns, June 1, 2021.

22. Heather Clark, "Clearwater Festival to Be Held Virtually for a Second Year in a Row: How to Watch," *Poughkeepsie Journal*, April 8, 2021.

23. Clark, "Clearwater Festival."

24. Author interview with Andy Bernstein, director of Headcount, May 2021.

25. Author interview with Si Kahn, March 2022.

26. Si Kahn, March 2022.

27. Author interview with Joan Kuyek, June 15, 2021. Kuyek is a researcher for MiningWatch, which published her report entitled "Behind the Pebble Mine: Hunter Dickinson Inc.; The Canadian Mining Company You've Never Heard Of," February 28, 2018.

28. Bonnie Gestring, "When It Comes to Pebble Mine: No Means No," *Earthworks*, June 28, 2018.

29. Author interview with Joel Reynolds, western director and senior attorney for NRDC, June 22, 2021.

30. Dino Gradoni, "EPA Proposes Protection for World's Biggest Sockeye Salmon Fishery," *Washington Post*, May 25, 2022.

31. Author interview with Jackson Browne via video call, February 24, 2022.

32. Rob Rosenthal and Richard Flacks, *Playing for Change: Music and Musicians in the Service of Social Movements* (Oxfordshire: Routledge), 126.

33. Author interview with Jasiri X, June 18, 2021.

34. Author interview with Bill McKibben, November 2, 2021.

35. Author interview with Denis Hayes, May 4, 2021.

36. Bill McKibben, "What the Warming World Needs Now Is Art, Sweet Art," *Grist*, April 22, 2005.

37. Havstad notes five distinct but interrelated issues that surface: (1) some artists and organizers never learned how to strategically couple art and poli-

tics, (2) institutions within the music industry and within the organizing community don't inherently support collaborative practices between artists and organizers, (3) siloed funding streams offer grants for advocacy or art but usually not for their integration, (4) racial and cultural gaps exist between those leading environmental organizations and those who are most affected by environmental issues, and (5) merging the different interests of movement leaders, who are focused on advocacy and organizing, and the music industry, which does not prioritize political impact. Author interview with Liz Havstad, June 8 and 28, 2021.

38. Liz Havstad, June 8 and 28, 2021.

39. Author interview with Liz Havstad, July 7, 2022.

40. Liz Havstad, July 7, 2022.

41. Author interview with Rev. Yearwood, June 11, 2021.

42. Rev. Yearwood, June 11, 2021.

43. Rev. Yearwood, June 11, 2021.

44. Quoted from the Highsnobiety website; www.highsnobiety.com/p/standing-rock-native-american-hip-hop.

45. Neil Young, "Indian Givers," https://www.youtube.com/watch?v=_O1uQOpzvPQ.

46. "Jason Mraz Joins Jackson Browne and Bonnie Raitt for a Benefit Concert at Standing Rock to Stand in Solidarity with Standing Rock," PRNewswire, November 10, 2016.

47. Rosenthal and Flacks, *Playing for Change*, 144.

3: Moving Images

1. Quoted in Paul VanDeCarr, *Storytelling and Social Change*, Working Narratives, Narrative Arts, 2016, narrativearts.org/wp-content/uploads/2016/02/story-guide-second-edition.pdf.

2. *The China Syndrome* premiered on March 16, 1979. The Three Mile Island meltdown occurred March 28, 1979. See www.imdb.com/title/tt0078966/releaseinfo and the U.S. Nuclear Regulatory Commission Library collection at www.nrc.gov/reading-rm/doc-collections/fact-sheets/3mile-isle.html.

3. For an overview of *The China Syndrome*, including details about the box office, awards, and ratings, see www.imdb.com.

4. David Burnham, "Nuclear Experts Debate 'The China Syndrome,'" *New York Times*, March 18, 1979.

5. Author interview with Jane Fonda, September 5, 2019.

6. Author interview with Pamela Yates and Paco de Onís, February 27, 2021.

7. *9to5: The Story of a Movement*, a documentary film directed and produced by Julia Reichert and Steven Bognar, released by PBS Distribution, February 1, 2021.

8. Interview with Karen Nussbaum, April 9, 2021.

9. Karen Nussbaum, April 9, 2021.

10. Lynn Neary, "A Cup of Ambition and Endurance: 9 to 5 Unites Workers Across Decades," *Morning Edition*, NPR, July 11, 2019.

11. Neary, "A Cup of Ambition and Endurance."

12. 9to5 was founded in Boston in 1973 and then affiliated with SEIU.

13. Karen Nussbaum, April 9, 2021.

14. Author interview with Kartemquin founder Gordon Quinn, March 9, 2021.

15. Author correspondence with Patricia Aufderheide, August 26, 2021.

16. Sonya Childress and Bullock Brown, "The Documentary Future: A Call for Accountability," *Documentary*, July 2, 2020.

17. Author interview with Pamela Yates and Paco de Onís, February 27, 2021.

18. Author correspondence with Pamela Yates, March 2021.

19. Pamela Yates, March 2021. (The Constitutional Court vacated the verdict on procedural [not evidentiary] grounds.)

20. Pamela Yates, March 2021.

21. For a description of SolidariLabs, see Skylight's website, skylight.is/solidarilabs.

22. Author interview with Pamela Yates and Paco de Onís, February 27, 2021.

23. Author interview with Jess Search, February 17, 2021.

24. Drawn from the website of Doc Society, goodpitch.org/about.

25. Author correspondence with Jess Search, May 10, 2021.

26. "Impact Field Guide and Toolkit," Doc Society, 2019.

27. National Domestic Workers Alliance (NDWA), www.domesticworkers.org/about-ndwa.

28. "Domestic Work Should Receive Priority COVID Vaccine Access," Hand in Hand, The Domestic Employees Network, actionnetwork.org/forms/domestic-workers-should-receive-priority-covid-vaccine-access.

29. "From *The Help* to *Roma*, How the National Domestic Workers Alliance Is Transforming Narratives in Pop Culture," Pop Culture Collaborative Report, NDWA.

30. Author interview with Norman Lear, November 18, 2019.

31. Author correspondence with Kristina Mevs-Apgar, August 25, 2021.

32. Academy Awards Acceptance Speech database, aaspeechesdb.oscars.org/link/091-8.

33. Author interview with Kristina Mevs-Apgar, February 17, 2021.

34. "From *The Help* to *Roma*," 14.

35. Author correspondence with Larissa Rhoades, Chasing Ice Productions coordinator, June 14, 2022.

36. For a detailed campaign analysis, see the "Dear Congressman Tiberi Campaign Story and Impact Report," Exposure Labs, 2014.

37. "Dear Congressman Tiberi."

38. "Dear Congressman Tiberi."

39. Author interview with Sonya Childress, March 11, 2021.

40. Sonya Childress, March 11, 2021.

41. Sonya Childress, March 11, 2021.

42. Sonya Childress, March 11, 2021.

43. Randall Roberts, "Beyoncé Draws Outrage and Praise for Super Bowl Set," *Los Angeles Times*, February 8, 2016.

44. Jenna Wortham, "Beyoncé in Formation: Entertainer, Activist or Both?" *New York Times*, February 6, 2016.

45. Author correspondence with Sonya Childress, July 28, 2022.

46. Author interview with Sonya Childress, March 11, 2021.

47. Sonya Childress, March 11, 2021.

48. Author interview with Stanley Nelson, February 19, 2021.

4: "No Papers, No Fear"

1. Author interview with Pablo Alvarado, December 21, 2021.

2. Randall C. Archibold, "Arizona Enacts Stringent Law on Immigration," *New York Times*, April 23, 2010.

3. Brian Tashman, quoted on the ACLU website Speak Freely, August 22, 2017.

4. The Dream Act of 2021 (S.264) defines "Dreamers" as individuals who entered the United States before age eighteen in 2017 or earlier and who have lived continually in the United States since that time.

5. National Day Laborer Organizing Network (NDLON), ndlon.org/category/cartoons.

6. "Wake Me Up," directed by Alex Rivera, song by Aloe Blacc, www.youtube.com/watch?v=M_o6axAseak.

7. Excerpted from an NDLON video, October 11, 2016, http://losjornalerosdelnorte.com/videos/story-los-jornaleros-del-norte/.

8. Daniel Kraker, "Sound Strike Targets Arizona Immigration Law," *All Things Considered*, NPR, July 23, 2010.

9. "Undocumented Immigrants Launch Bus Tour," Arizona Public Radio, July 31, 2012.

10. Author interview with Pablo Alvarado, December 21, 2021.

11. Cultural strategy is a field of practice that centers artists, storytellers, media makers, musicians, and cultural influencers as agents of social change. See Erin Potts, Jeff Chang, and Liz Manne, "A Conversation About Cultural Strategy," in *A More Perfect Story*, Medium, June 15, 2018.

12. Author interview with Favianna Rodriguez, December 7, 2021. Operation Streamline was a government-run program that brought groups of migrants into a hearing and summarily issued mass deportation orders. The Florence Immigrant and Refugee Rights project provides free legal and social services to detained adults and children under threat of deportation.

13. Favianna Rodriguez, favianna.com/artworks/?categories=SJPT.

14. Brooke Park, "Artists Unveil Monarch Butterfly Mural at Linder Elementary in Austin," *Austin American-Statesman*, November 2, 2021.

15. According to reporting from *Harper's Bazaar*, more than two-thirds of the undocumented population work in essential industries, Chelsey Sanchez, April 29, 2021.

16. Mekita Rivas, in Shondaland, June 3, 2021.

17. Kevin Roose, "What Is QAnon, the Viral Pro-Trump Conspiracy Theory?" *New York Times*, September 3, 2021.

18. Rob Rosenthal and Richard Flacks, *Playing for Change: Music and Musicians in the Service of Social Movements* (Oxfordshire: Routledge), 8.

19. Amplifier-produced poster of Lizbeth Mateo Jimenez, designed by Ernesto Yerena Montejano.

20. Author interview with Cleo Barnett, co-creative director, Amplifier, 2021.

21. Claudia E. Zapata, Terezita Romo, E. Carmen Ramos, and Tatiana Reinoza, *¡Printing the Revolution! The Rise and Impact of Chicano Graphics, 1965 to Now*, ed. Carmen Ramos (Princeton, NJ: Princeton University Press, published in conjunction with the Smithsonian Art Museum exhibit by the same title, 2020), 145.

22. Author interview with Julio Salgado, January 8, 2022.

23. KQED interview by Herrick Wu, July 5, 2018.

24. Julio Salgado, January 8, 2022.

25. Tessa Solomon, "This Independence Weekend, 80 Artists Will Protest Immigrant Incarceration in Nationwide Skywriting Campaign," *ARTNews*, July 3, 2020.

26. Race Forward: The Center for Racial Justice Innovation, raceforward.org/practice/tools/drop-i-word.

27. Author interview with Jose Antonio Vargas, January 11, 2022.

28. Used with the permission of the author, Yosimar Reyes.

29. Author interview with Yosimar Reyes, January 11, 2022.

30. The Center for Cultural Power, discussed in more detail in chapter 6, organizes artists to engage in social action and manages a fund that supports this work.

31. Author interview with Jose Antonio Vargas, January 11, 2022.

32. Excerpted from "The Butterfly Lab for Immigration Narrative Strategy, Year 1 Findings," Race Forward, February 2022.

33. "Judy Baca's Murals Recover History Through 'Public Memory,'" video on the history of the Great Wall, *PBS NewsHour*, KCET, January 18, 2012.

34. Excerpted from "Inside Giants: Kikito on the U.S.-Mexican Border," JR's YouTube channel, February 28, 2020.

35. Alexandra Schwartz, "The Artist JR Lifts a Mexican Child over the Border Wall," *New Yorker*, September 11, 2017; Rory Carroll, "Proud to Be Mexican: Meet the Baby Whose Huge Image Gazes over the Border," *The Guardian*, September 18, 2017; David Bacon, "The Art of the Border: Searching for Kikito," *American Prospect*, October 30, 2017.

36. For this project, part of a global participatory art initiative, JR partnered with the Emerson Collective, which offers philanthropy and venture capital

for immigration reform, arts, and activism. The collective is funded by Laurene Powell Jobs.

37. As quoted on the Inside Out 11M website, photobooth.insideoutproject.net/project/28-Inside-Out-11M.

38. Inside Out 11M.

39. Author interview with Hank Willis Thomas, June 27, 2019.

40. Author interview with Jeff Chang, January 22, 2022.

41. Author interview with Shepard Fairey, December 10, 2020.

42. Cristina Costantini, February 27, 2013, *ABC News*.

5: "You Can't Be Neutral on a Moving Train"

1. David Gelles, "Smithsonian's Leader Says Museums Have a Social Justice Role to Play," *New York Times*, July 2, 2020.

2. Robin Pogrebin, "Breaking Down Barriers at MoMA's PS1 in Queens," *New York Times*, April 9, 2022.

3. Pogrebin, "Breaking Down Barriers."

4. Holland Cotter, "Money, Ethics, Art: Can Museums Police Themselves?" *New York Times*, May 9, 2019.

5. Author interview with Naila Caicedo-Rosario and Tom Finkelpearl, March 4, 2022.

6. U.S. Census Bureau 2010, Census Public Law 97-171 File Population Division, New York City Department of City Planning, March 29, 2011. See www1.nyc.gov/assets/planning/download/pdf/data-maps/nyc-population/census2010/t_pl_p3a_nta.pdf.

7. Excerpted from Valeria Mogilevich, Mariana Mogilevich and Queens Museum staff, Prerana Reddy, María Alexandra García, and José Serrano-McClain, "Corona Plaza es Para Todos: Making a Dignified Public Space for Immigrants," Queens Museum of Art, 2016.

8. Queens Museum of Art website, queensmuseum.org/corona-plaza.

9. Official website of the New York City Department of Parks and Recreation. See www.nycgovparks.org/art/art42.

10. New York City Department of Parks and Recreation.

11. Author interview with Miki Garcia, April 2022.

12. Miki Garcia, April 2022.

13. Collen Dilenschneider, "People Trust Museums More than Newspapers.

Here Is Why That Matters," from "Impacts Experience" polling featured on the author's website, April 2017, www.collendilen.com.

14. Wynton Marsalis interview with Bryan Stevenson, presented as an exhibition in the Legacy Museum.

15. EJI online video discussing the cultural complex.

16. See the Equal Justice Initiative at eji.org/projects/community-remembrance-project.

17. Campbell Robertson, "A Lynching Memorial Is Opening. The Country Has Never Seen Anything Like It," *New York Times*, April 25, 2018.

18. "Museum Board Leadership: A National Report," American Alliance of Museums, January 19, 2018, www.aam-us.org/2018/01/19/museum-board-leadership-2017-a-national-report/.

19. Geoffrey Dunn, "How Nina Simon Reinvented Santa Cruz Art," *Good Times*, June 4, 2019.

20. Drawn from the American Museum of Natural History website, www.amnh.org/research/richard-gilder-graduate-school/school-overview/the-museum-s-mission#:~:text=To%20discover%2C%20interpret%2C%20and%20disseminate,natural%20world%2C%20and%20the%20universe.

21. Author interview with Beka Economopoulos, April 8, 2022.

22. Laura Raicovich, *Culture Strike: Art and Museums in an Age of Protest* (London: Verso, 2021), 22.

23. Author interview with Beka Economopoulos, March 13, 2022.

24. Beka Economopoulos, March 13, 2022.

25. Author correspondence with Allison Barlow from the Wallace Global Fund, April 2022.

26. Author correspondence with Beka Economopoulos, July 19, 2022.

27. Beka Economopoulos, July 19, 2022.

28. Carlie Poterfield, "Sacklers Agree to $6 Billion Settlement of Opioid Litigation Involving Their Pharma Purdue," *Forbes*, September 1, 2021.

29. Peggy McGlone, "The Sacklers Have Donated Millions to Museums. But Their Connection to the Opioid Crisis Is Threatening That Legacy," *Washington Post*, February 13, 2019.

30. Leslie Albrecht, "Sackler Family Banned—Temporarily—from Putting Their Name on Buildings as Part of $4.5 Billion Opioid Settlement," *MarketWatch*, July 13, 2021.

31. Kara Swisher, "How the Sacklers Got Away with It," an interview with author Patrick Radden Keefe, *New York Times*, February 14, 2022.

32. Alex Marshall, "British Museum to Remove Sackler Name from its Walls," *New York Times*, March 25, 2022.

33. Prizewinning author Emily Bingham published a book about the controversial lyrics and history of the song called *My Old Kentucky Home: The Astonishing Life and Reckoning of an Iconic American Song* (New York: Alfred Knopf, 2022).

34. The Kentucky Derby reinstated the performance with full marching band and choir in 2022, wfpl.org/my-old-kentucky-home-will-be-performed-at-the-derby-this-weekend-by-a-marching-band-and-choir.

35. Author email correspondence with Martha Slaughter, May 2, 2022.

36. Author interview with Sadiqa Reynolds, June 7, 2022.

37. Author interview with Stephen Reily, May 4, 2022.

38. Author correspondence with Amy Sherald, November 16, 2022.

39. Holland Cotter, "Breonna Taylor Show Puts Art Museums on a Faster Track," *New York Times*, April 14, 2021.

40. Siddhartha Mitter, "How a Museum Show Honoring Breonna Taylor Is Trying to 'Get it Right,'" *New York Times*, March 11, 2021.

41. Mitter, "Museum Show."

42. Brian Boucher, "In a Landslide Decision, Workers at the Museum of Fine Arts in Boston Have Become the Latest Major US Museum Staff to Unionize," *Artnet*, November 23, 2020, news.artnet.com/art-world/mfa-boston-union-1925848.

43. Alex Greenberger, "'It's Helpful to Know All Scales': Online Spreadsheet Discloses Museum Workers' Salaries," *ARTnews*, May 31, 2019, www.artnews.com/art-news/news/google-spreadsheet-museum-workers-disclose-salaries-12670.

44. Zachery Small, "U.S. Museums See Rise in Unions Even as Labor Movement Slumps," *New York Times*, February 21, 2022.

45. Small, "Rise in Unions."

46. Jason Fargo, "Glen Lowry, MoMA Director, Will Continue Through 2025," *New York Times*, November 16, 2018.

6: Toward Art, Activism, and Transformative Philanthropy

1. Michael Eric Dyson, *Come Hell or High Water: Hurricane Katrina and the Color of Disaster* (New York: Basic Civtas, 2007).

2. Author interview with Catherine Gund, October 21, 2021.

3. Robin Pogrebin, "Agnes Gund Sells a Lichtenstein to Start Criminal Justice Fund," *New York Times*, June 11, 2017.

4. Darren Walker and Elizabeth Alexander, *From Generosity to Justice, a New Gospel of Wealth* (New York: Ford Foundation/Disruption Books, 2019).

5. Holly Sidford, *Fusing Art, Culture and Social Change*, National Committee for Responsive Philanthropy (NCRP), 7, October 23, 2011.

6. Although BLM did not receive a lot of "upfront" support, it subsequently raised more than $40 million through its 501(c)(3) foundation. See www.knkx.org/social-justice/2022-05-17/black-lives-matter-foundation-has-42-million-in-assets. Occupy Wall Street contributions came largely from individual donors and labor organizations, owing in part to the relatively short duration of the movement and the lack of rapid response capacity among institutional donors.

7. Crystal Hayling, "Transformative Philanthropy for Racial Justice," *Stanford Social Innovation Review* (Fall 2021).

8. Author interview Maurine Knighton, May 3, 2022. Knighton succeeded Claudine Brown as the Cummings Art and Culture program director.

9. Pam Korza and Barbara Schaffer Bacon, *Trend or Tipping Point: Arts and Social Change Grantmaking: A 2010 Report and Resource for Funders* (Washington, DC: Americans for the Arts, 2010).

10. Author interview with Michelle Coffey, April 22, 2022.

11. This blog post and news story are no longer available online.

12. Justin George, Ian Duncan, and Carrie Wells, "Group Targets Baltimore Vacants with Art, Activism," *Baltimore Sun*, August 9, 2013.

13. Baynard Woods, "Wall Hunters Takes on the Slumlords Crippling Baltimore Neighborhoods," *Baltimore City Paper*, September 4, 2013.

14. Edward Erickson Jr., "The Sun's Credulous Take on Stanly Rochkind," *Baltimore City Paper*, June 4, 2014.

15. Yvonne Wenger, "City to Raze Hundreds of Vacant Houses in Stepped-Up Plan," *Baltimore Sun*, August 15, 2013.

16. This article, "Street Art Gives Voice to the Community on Low-Income

Housing," was written by the author and appeared in GIA's online journal, *Grantmakers in the Arts*, www.giarts.org/article/street-art-gives-voice-community-low-income-housing.

17. Ed Fuentes, "Monthly Mural Wrap: A Dozen Tags for March 2014," KCET, March 5, 2014.

18. Author correspondence with Arlene Goldbard, citing her 2009 paper "Cultural Recovery."

19. Liz Manne, Rachel D. Godsil, Mik Moore, Meredith Osborne, Joseph Phelan, Thelma Adams, Michael Ahn, Brian Sheppard, *Pop Justice: Volume 1: Social Justice and the Promise of Pop Culture Strategies*, Liz Manne Strategy, February 2016.

20. Manne et al., *Pop Justice*.

21. Author interview with Norman Lear, November 18, 2019.

22. Norman Lear, November 18, 2019.

23. Lin-Manuel Miranda, as told to Frank Digiacomo, "'Hamilton's' Lin-Manuel Miranda on Finding Originality, Racial Politics (and Why Trump Should See His Show)," *Hollywood Reporter*, August 12, 2015.

24. Ginger Daniel, *#MakingJusticePop: The Story of the Pop Culture Collaborative's Impact at 5 Years*, Pop Culture Collaborative, March 2022.

25. John Anderson, "Relinquishing Purse Strings," *New York Times*, February 15, 2013.

26. Author interview with Cara Mertes, April 27, 2022.

27. See the Art for Justice Fund website for more detail, artforjusticefund.org/faqs.

28. The fund subsequently added a sixth additional year of distributions because it received additional funding, largely, but not exclusively, from the art world.

29. Author interview with Catherine Gund, October 21, 2021.

30. Author correspondence with Helena Huang, July 25, 2022.

31. Cultural strategy as defined by the Constellations fund is a "field of practice that centers artists, storytellers, media makers and cultural influencers as agents of change." Organizational document, 2020.

32. Author interview with Javier Torres-Campos, October 20, 2021.

33. Author interview with Helena Huang, October 2021.

34. Fang Block, "Julie Mehretu's Dissident Score Sells via Artsy for U.S.

$6.5 million, a Record for the Artist," *Barron's*, June 11, 2021; Ford Foundation president Darren Walker's interview with Julie Mehretu, May 26, 2021.

35. The Needmor Fund is a foundation that supports grassroots community organizing.

36. Author interview with Javier Torres-Campos, October 20, 2021.

37. 501(c)(3) is an IRS designation for a nonprofit organization. A 501(c)(4) is an IRS designated social welfare organization. Both the Open Philanthropy Project Fund and the Open Philanthropy Action Fund support a wide range of issue work, including criminal justice reform.

38. Author interview with Chloe Cockburn, November 12, 2021.

39. Author interview with Denis Hayes, May 3, 2021.

40. For more information about the Fundred project, see the artist's website, fundred.org.

41. Mel Chin in conversation with organizers and artist-activists, June 28, 2022, hosted by the author.

42. Neda Ulaby, "Artist in Residence Creates Portraits of Reform at the District Attorney's Office," *Arts Desk*, NPR, October 19, 2020.

43. See the Brennan Center report, *Voting Rights Restoration Efforts in Florida: A Summary of Current Felony Disenfranchisement Policies and Legislative Advocacy in Florida*, www.brennancenter.org/our-work/research-reports/voting-rights-restoration-efforts-florida.

44. Lawrence Mower, "She Owes $59 Million. Should She Be Allowed to Vote Under Amendment 4?," *Tampa Bay Times*, March 25, 2019. Leicht's case was also cited in court documents in the *Kelvin Jones v. DeSantis* lawsuit, March 2, 2020.

45. Author interview with Desmond Meade, December 1, 2021.

46. Author correspondence with Helena Huang, July 27, 2022.

47. This is a conservative figure representing the number of formerly incarcerated individuals who had legal financial obligations to the state for which public records could be found. It is likely there were many more records of the formerly incarcerated that could not be found, as this information is not collected by each county. Derived from extensive research by University of Florida expert Daniel Smith, PhD, 774,000 is the number of disenfranchised that is cited in the court documents for *Kelvin Jones v. DeSantis*, March 2, 2020.

48. Author interview with Dana Bourland, December 8, 2021.

7: Afterword

1. Sonya Childress worked as an Impact producer for fourteen years at Firelight Media, a nonprofit organization that supports and develops nonfiction filmmakers of color. She recently served as a senior fellow with the Perspective Fund and is co-founder of Color Congress, a national collective of majority people of color (POC) and POC-led organizations aimed at centering and strengthening nonfiction storytelling by, for, and about people of color across the United States and its territories.

2. Jasiri X is the founder and CEO of One Hood Media, whose mission is to build liberated communities through art, education, and social justice. His critically acclaimed album *Black Liberation Theology* (2015) has been recognized as a soundtrack for today's civil rights movement, and he is the first independent hip-hop artist to receive an honorary doctorate from the Chicago Theological Seminary, in 2016.

3. Josie Mooney has a thirty-five-year career working in movements for social change. She's worked as a community organizer, was a longtime senior official at SEIU, and worked with People's Action and Tom Steyer at NextGen. She was the first woman president of the San Francisco Labor Council and led the group for nearly a decade. Currently, Mooney serves as deputy director of an SEIU local and oversees organizing, communications, research, and politics.

4. Shepard Fairey is an artist-activist who may be best known for his HOPE poster of Barack Obama, found today at the Smithsonian Portrait Gallery, for the "We the People" series, recognizable in women's marches and other rallies worldwide, and his "Obey" street work. After more than thirty years, his work has evolved into an acclaimed body of art. He's painted 110 large-scale murals across six continents worldwide.

5. Mel Chin is a conceptual artist whose work over the last thirty-five years has ranged widely and includes organizing national and local organizations and communities to remediate lead in soil, in the Fundred Project, and investigating how art can promote greater awareness and responsibility through popular television.

6. George Goehl is among the most highly recognized community organizers in the nation, having served as executive director of People's Action and the host of two podcasts, *The Next Move* and *To See Each Other.* He is a husband, father, and banjo player and makes documentaries about country music.

7. Michael Premo is a multidisciplinary artist, journalist, and documentary

storyteller. He is co-founder and executive producer of Storyline, which creates award-winning documentaries in multiple mediums: film, photography, audio/radio/oral history, and live installations.

8. Aisha Shillingford worked for twenty years as an Alinsky-trained organizer. She is an artist and the artistic director of Intelligent Mischief, " a creative studio and future designs lab using art, entertainment, and experiences to develop transformative cultural strategies that unleash Black imagination to shape the future."

9. The music video supported the Color of Change campaign (and others) to demand justice for Trayvon. It was seen by more than 193,000 viewers in 2012 and more since, www.youtube.com/watch?v=YKaJoEyYXyI.

10. From 1995 to 1997, on network television's prime-time soap opera *Melrose Place*, the GALA committee sought to work with commercial television by actively approaching it as a proper site in which to develop possibilities for education, to generate the transfer of information, and to layer narratives and poetic constructions. For the fuller scope of Chin's work on *Melrose Place*, see melchin.org/oeuvre/in-the-name-of-the-place.

INDEX OF NAMES

References to plates refer to the color insert between pages 79 and 80 of the text; page numbers in italic refer to images in the main text.

ABOUT THE AUTHOR

Ken Grossinger has been a leading strategist in movements for social and economic justice for thirty-five years, in unions and community organizations, and as director of Impact Philanthropy in Democracy Partners. Among other cultural projects, he co-executive produced the award-winning Netflix documentaries *Social Dilemma* and *Bleeding Edge*. He lives in Washington, DC.

PUBLISHING IN THE PUBLIC INTEREST

Thank you for reading this book published by The New Press; we hope you enjoyed it. New Press books and authors play a crucial role in sparking conversations about the key political and social issues of our day.

We hope that you will stay in touch with us. Here are a few ways to keep up to date with our books, events, and the issues we cover:

- Sign up at www.thenewpress.com/subscribe to receive updates on New Press authors and issues and to be notified about local events
- www.facebook.com/newpressbooks
- www.twitter.com/thenewpress
- www.instagram.com/thenewpress

Please consider buying New Press books not only for yourself, but also for friends and family and to donate to schools, libraries, community centers, prison libraries, and other organizations involved with the issues our authors write about.

The New Press is a 501(c)(3) nonprofit organization; if you wish to support our work with a tax-deductible gift, please visit www.thenewpress.com/donate or use the QR code below.